Meet God Again

Other books by this author:

The Day That Changed the World (Pacific Press)
The Millennium Bug (Pacific Press)
Present Truth in the Real World (Pacific Press)
What the Bible Says About the End-time

To order, call
1-800-765-6955.

Visit us at
www.reviewandherald.com
for information on other Review and Herald® products.

JON PAULIEN

REVIEW AND HERALD® PUBLISHING ASSOCIATION
HAGERSTOWN, MD 21740

Copyright © 2003 by
Review and Herald® Publishing Association
All rights reserved

The author assumes full responsibility for the accuracy of all facts and quotations as cited in this book.

Unless otherwise noted, Bible texts are from the *Holy Bible, New International Version*. Copyright © 1973, 1978, 1984, International Bible Society. Used by permission of Zondervan Bible Publishers.

This book was
Edited by Gerald Wheeler
Copyedited by Delma Miller and James Cavil
Cover designed by Square 1 Studio
Cover photo by Photos.com
Interior designed by Trent Truman
Electronic makeup by Shirley M. Bolivar
Typeset: Bembo 12/15

PRINTED IN U.S.A.

07 06 05 04 03   5 4 3 2 1

R&H Cataloging Service
Paulien, Jon, 1949-
    Meet God again for the first time.

    1. Bible—Study and teaching.   I. Title.

            220.7

ISBN 0-8280-1768-9

CONTENTS

INTRODUCTION 9

—PART ONE—
The Bible and the Power of History

CHAPTER   1: Retell Me the Good Old Story 17
CHAPTER   2: How It All Began 22
CHAPTER   3: Israel as a Nation 37
CHAPTER   4: Exile and Return 45
CHAPTER   5: The Pattern of New Testament Faith .. 55

—PART TWO—
The Bible and the Rules of Relationship

CHAPTER   6: Designed for Stability 79
CHAPTER   7: The Old Testament Concept of Law ... 89
CHAPTER   8: The New Testament Concept of Law . 99

—PART THREE—
The Bible and Everyday Experience

CHAPTER   9: A New History 115
CHAPTER 10: A New Relationship With God 126
CHAPTER 11: A New Way to Live 137

PREFACE

No one is an island, and no worthwhile book is the product of a single mind. I would be remiss, therefore, if I didn't acknowledge the role that many people played in my journey toward the insights about God and getting right with God that you will find in this book.

There is no better path toward truth than open conversation, and I am grateful to many conversation partners who have knowingly or unknowingly invested in my life. I include in this group of partners people I have known face to face and others I have known only through books.

I grew up in a Seventh-day Adventist home, so my first mentor regarding God and salvation was Ellen G. White through Spirit-filled books such as *Steps to Christ, Thoughts From the Mount of Blessing, The Desire of Ages,* and *The Ministry of Healing.* While most people who know her writings seem to give pride of place to the book *Steps to Christ,* for me the absolute high point of her writings on salvation are to be found in *Thoughts From the Mount of Blessing* (pages 6-21), *The Desire of Ages,* and *The Ministry of Healing* (pages 51-107).

As I reached young adulthood and entered the pastorate, I was especially grateful for the personal attentions of such spiritual stalwarts as Charles Sohlmann, Jim Londis, Hans LaRondelle, Ivan Blazen, and Raoul Dederen, the last three of whom were my teachers at Andrews University. During this same period two books were instrumental in leading me to a full, personal commitment to Jesus Christ: Glenn Coon's *Path to the Heart* (Washington, D.C.: Review and Herald, 1958) and Robert Brinsmead's *Pattern of Redemptive History* (Fallbrook, Calif.: Verdict Publications, 1979). While the author may no longer agree with what he wrote then, you will find some echoes of the latter book in this one.

As I began my teaching ministry at Andrews University in the 1980s, several more books enticed me into dialogue on this subject. I will list four of them here, with Gage's book being, perhaps, the greatest single influence on the content of the book you hold in your hand: Ada R. Habershon, *Hidden Pictures in the Old Testament,* reprint of the 1916 original (Grand Rapids: Kregel Publications, 1982); Graeme Goldsworthy, *Gospel and Kingdom: A Christian's Guide to the Old Testament* (Minneapolis: Winston Press, 1981); Warren Austin Gage, *The Gospel of Genesis: Studies in Protology and Eschatology* (Winona Lake, Ind.: Carpenter Books, 1984); and John R. W. Stott, *The Cross of Christ* (Downer's Grove, Ill.: InterVarsity Press, 1986).

In the 1990s I have been particularly blessed by Alister McGrath, *The Mystery of the Cross* (Grand Rapids: Zondervan Publishing House, 1988), C. S. Lewis, *Mere Christianity* (New York: The Macmillan Co., 1960); Richard Hays, *Echoes of Scripture in the Letters of Paul* (New Haven, Conn.: Yale University Press, 1989); and N. T. Wright, *The Climax of the Covenant* (Minneapolis: Fortress Press, 1992).

None of the above should be blamed for the final shape of my book. Its flaws and its focus are truly my own. And it is, above all, an attempt to understand the Bible, which is the primary source of what you will read on the pages that follow. But I will always be grateful for these other friends and the roles they played at crucial points in my life. I have had many other teachers, but these are the ones who most helped to make this particular book possible.

INTRODUCTION

JESUS IS THE ANSWER?

One day I was driving down an interstate highway minding my own business when a strategically placed billboard interrupted my random thoughts. "Jesus Is the Answer," it proclaimed loudly in giant letters. Nothing more. No explanation. Not even a hint as to what the question might be.

No doubt whoever commissioned the billboard would tell you that the Bible explains both the answer and the question. Does that make you feel any better? Or does it make you want to run for cover? After all, didn't many of the Nazis read their Bibles (at the time society considered Germany a "Christian" nation)? Didn't many South Africans think the Bible supported apartheid? Wasn't David Koresh studying his Bible right up to the day the Waco compound burned down? Can't you find anything you want to find in the Bible? All these things are true—up to a point. Let me illustrate.

One day a young man tried to get some help from the Bible. He hadn't spent much time studying his Bible through the years, but now he needed some answers. So he employed an interesting method (he wasn't the first). After praying that God would guide him, he picked up a Bible and dropped it on a table, allowing it to fall open without his looking at it. He then placed his finger on the open pages and looked to see what God might be saying to him. He read: "Judas went out and hanged himself." Not only was the answer depressing; it didn't seem to have a lot to do with his question! So he decided to try the method again. This time the text he pointed to said: "Go and do likewise." Now the message was getting clearer, but he wasn't too thrilled with the direction things were going. So he thought he would use the method one more time to see if he could get it right. Again he dropped his Bible and put his finger on a text. This time he read: "What you are doing, do quickly." What this outrageous story demonstrates is that you can put Bible texts together to prove anything you want to.

WHAT DO YOU MEAN, "I DON'T GET IT"?

Is that all then? Is there no point in even trying to understand what the Bible is all about? Interestingly, the Bible itself offers some serious cautions about the limits of human research. Jeremiah 17:9 declares: "The heart is deceitful above all things and beyond cure. Who can understand it?" A passage that ought to disturb anyone who thinks they understand the Bible, it suggests that self-deceptive mechanisms lurk inside every one of us that blind us to the way things really are. They work in service of an internal "spin doctor" (the heart) that protects our psyche from stuff we don't really want to know. Psychologists call such self-deceptive techniques defense mechanisms. We have a natural bent to distort reality and to avoid the truth about ourselves.

Let me illustrate how defense mechanisms work. Suppose I am teaching in a large classroom when Randy Johnson walks in with a baseball in his hand. For those who never heard of him, six-foot-10-inch Randy Johnson makes a good living throwing baseballs 101 miles per hour! He's somewhat scary-looking, too. Suppose he took exception to something I told the class and launched his 101-mile-per-hour fastball right toward my nose? Would I stop teaching and ponder my response? *Well, let's see, Randy Johnson just launched a 100-mile-an-hour fastball toward my nose. I suppose I should start thinking about getting out of the way.* I don't think so! Much faster than you can say "Randy Johnson" I would have my hands up in front of my face to block his attack on my life! I wouldn't need to think about it. In fact, I wouldn't even be conscious I had reacted until after I felt the sting of the baseball on my wrists. The response would be automatic.

Just as we have natural defense mechanisms at the physical level, so also we have them at the emotional and psychological level. If someone says something hurtful about us, we may react without even being aware that we have done so. We quickly protect our honor and reputation even when we argue loud and long that we are not acting defensive!

At a basic level, then, such defense mechanisms are self-deceptions. When things go wrong, when we fail at something important, or when we are under verbal or emotional attack, we instantly do everything possible to safeguard our sense of security, whether we intend to or not. Defense mechanisms help us avoid feeling bad about ourselves. And if knowing the truth is going to make us feel bad about ourselves, most of us would prefer not to know the truth.

The greater the perceived threat, the more rapid and thorough the response. So we shouldn't be surprised that when we open the Bible, faced with the ultimate threat (God), our defense mechanisms go into warp drive. People distort the message of the Bible out of a need to protect their own feelings and ideas from a higher authority. If you can't beat Him, reinterpret Him! Perhaps that is one reason there are so many different churches, all claiming to follow the Bible.

What should we do? Quit trying to understand ourselves or the higher realities of the universe? I'm not sure that we could do so even if we wanted to. Something about the human spirit drives us to ask questions and demand answers. And throughout history, hundreds of millions of people have found the Jesus of the Bible to be the answer to life's deepest questions. Many of them have been willing to die for the things that they have learned from the Bible. It makes sense that we give it a serious shot for ourselves, at least once. I'm inviting you to do it now, using this book as a guide.

GETTING THE BIG PICTURE

Is there a way to read the Bible that will leave us more open to its message? Can we avoid making the mistakes that so many others have committed as they contemplated its pages? A good way to understand any book is to spend time with its author. So it is helpful to invite God, the ultimate author of the Bible, to be present as we read His Book. If anyone can help us understand, it is the author of the Book.

The next step is to approach the Bible in a way quite different from that of the young man who thought the Bible was telling him to commit suicide. It involves taking a big-picture approach to the text. To look for the flow of what is actually happening in the Bible, rather than seeking to impose our own concepts on the text. It is to be open to the whole Bible, as it reads, rather than picking and choosing what looks good to us at first glance. And it is to ground one's understanding on what is clear in Scripture rather than trying to make the more obscure things say what we want them to.

How did I learn this method? One day in Brooklyn, New York, I had a visit from a Jehovah's Witness. I decided to spend some time studying the Bible with him to see what his group believed. As you might expect, we disagreed about every Bible text that we looked at. In frustration one day I suggested something radical. "If the Bible is the ultimate source of truth," I commented, "then no organization should be allowed to control what the Bible says."

Finally we agreed on something! So we decided to lay aside all books and articles about the Bible and read just the New Testament (the part of the Bible that focuses most directly on the story of Jesus) through from beginning to end. When we finished, we each asked ourselves the question "Do my beliefs reflect the central themes of the New Testament or do they mirror what someone else has taught me?" We both discovered that the Bible, broadly read, is a very different book from what it seems to be when one takes a text here and a text there and then puts them together.

Now, I don't know what our encounter did for that Jehovah's Witness in the long run, but I know it changed my life. I learned to test every opinion I held about the Bible with the plain teachings of the text in its widest context. When I began to do this, I became amazed at what I had missed. The Bible became a very different book than the one I had thought I already knew. The result of 20 years of such Bible study is what you will find in this book.

By all means, test what you learn here by the biblical text itself. When you have finished this book, do your own reading of Scripture. Read the big picture of the Bible for yourself, not just a little here and a little there. Don't judge my book by what you already think. Test it by what the Bible actually says. If you are already active in a church or have spent a lot of time with the Bible, I invite you to do what that Jehovah's Witness was willing to do. Lay aside everything you have ever heard about the Bible and approach it fresh, as if for the first time. I think you will be amazed at what you have missed. If you are not a Christian and don't know much about the Bible, count yourself lucky! In some ways you will have an easier time following the rest of this book than will someone who already knows a lot about Scripture.

The goal and purpose of this book is to understand both the question and the answer implied in that billboard I mentioned at the beginning of this introduction. Reading this book will introduce you to the Jesus I never knew growing up in a Christian home. In an age when terrorists commit unspeakable acts we need to know whether or not God is up to His job. I believe that reading this book will bring you the picture of a mighty God who is alive and well today. Though it may bring you into previously uncharted waters, reading this book will be a life-changing adventure!

PART ONE

The Bible and the Power of History

CHAPTER 1

RETELL ME THE GOOD OLD STORY

First Impressions

First impressions can make a big difference in the way you think of someone or something. When I first met Gaspar, I thought not only that he was not very good-looking but also that he appeared rather sneaky and underhanded. My initial impressions seemed confirmed when he went after my own girlfriend. The rat! In his defense, I must admit that she started it by inviting him to the girls'-invite banquet to make a point with me—the poor guy found himself caught in the middle! But at the time I was in no mood to be charitable.

The fascinating thing is that we became friends in the wake of that incident. He eventually became my college roommate and then my best and most trusted friend. I came to realize that my first impressions about him were totally wrong (he even got better-looking as he got older!). I'm glad that my first impressions of him did not govern our relationship permanently.

First impressions of the Bible are not always accurate either. So as we start our biblical journey together I'd like to invite you to forget everything you've ever heard or thought about the Bible for a while. Let the message of the Bible have a fresh opportunity to impact your life. You won't be sorry that you did.

When you open a Bible for the first time you find that most of it consists of a series of books collectively called the Old Testament. The Old Testament is filled with poetry and song, prophecy and proverb, but mainly narrative—a story of sorts. What does that story tell us about God? How did people back then find peace with Him and within themselves? What difference can that make in our lives today?

At first glance the Old Testament as a whole reads like a national history. It describes the ups and downs of one people's political and economic fortunes. But it is more than just an ordinary history. For one thing, it goes back past the founding fathers all the way to the creation of the world. The very first chapters set the stage for the national story, telling us about events no human could have witnessed, and no human historian could have described without supernatural aid.

The biblical narrative tells the story of how God made a perfect world way back in the beginning. Next it explains how this perfect world changed with the introduction of strife and violence. Out of this evil world God called Abraham to be the father of a nation, to follow Him and be His channel of benefit to all the nations (Gen. 12:1-3). The rest of the Old Testament (from Genesis 12 until the end) primarily concerns the history of this people called Israel. More than this, the Old Testament relates the history of a nation in constant interaction with God. And it focuses less on what the nation does than on what God does to and for that nation. As one writer put it, the Old Testament is the book of the acts of God.

An Active God

This active God may surprise you. Contrary to what many people assume, the Bible is not primarily about rules regulating behavior but about the Person behind those rules. People have often stayed away from the Bible because they don't want some big guy in the sky telling them what to do. But in the Bible we come to know God by what He does as much as by what He says. The Word of God is as much His *actions* as it is His words.

This fact is vital for us today. Most people believe in God, but question whether He is active in their lives or in the contemporary affairs of nations. They wonder if He set the world in motion and then went on vacation. But the Bible portrays a God who is active in history and in personal experience. And that is just the kind of God who can make a difference in our individual lives.

This emphasis on God's action is very typical of Hebrew thinking (Hebrew was the language of ancient Israel). In the developed world today we are accustomed to abstract thinking about ideas, including concepts such as love, truth, beauty, and liberty. But in Bible times Hebrews expressed their spiritual concerns in practical, everyday terms. Notice the expressions in an ancient confession of faith:

"In the future, when your son asks you, 'What is the meaning of the stipulations, decrees and laws the Lord our God has commanded you?' tell him: 'We were slaves of Pharaoh in Egypt, but the Lord brought us out of Egypt with a mighty hand. Before our eyes the Lord sent miraculous signs and wonders—great and terrible—upon Egypt and Pharaoh and his whole household. But he brought us out from there to bring us in and give us the land that he promised on oath to our forefathers. The Lord commanded us to obey all these decrees and to fear the Lord our God, so that we might always prosper and be kept alive, as is the case today. And if we are careful to obey all this law before the Lord our God, as he has commanded us, that will be our righteousness'" (Deut. 6:20-25).

This passage answers the basic questions of life by describing what God has done in highly practical terms. And what He expected His people to do in turn was equally concrete and practical. God wanted them to "obey," to do the right thing, to respond to His actions for them. But this matter of obedience is not about arbitrary rules and regulations. God's laws are reflections of what He does. So the Bible's message about what He has done for us and how we are to respond is very practical—it is about action more than it is about how we think or what we believe.

An Active Response

In Old Testament times the most important way to respond to God was through worship. But the Hebrew concept of worship differs greatly from ours. We often think of worship as an event at which some preacher tries to tell us what to do. But worship for them was not about human obligations, rather about what God had done—a recounting of His acts. "He has caused his wonders to be remembered; the Lord is gracious and compassionate" (Ps. 111:4). When the Hebrews told and retold the stories of what God had done, they identified with what had happened, became part of it, and then belonged to that history.

The Old Testament offers many examples of such a retelling. One of my favorites is Psalm 78. It contains 72 verses recounting God's acts in Israel's history. Telling how the people passed the story from generation to generation, it describes at length the Exodus, the plagues, the Red Sea, the wilderness wandering, and the Promised Land (verses 12-55). It depicts the trials of the period of the judges (verses 56-64), then concludes in triumph with David and the Temple (verses 65-72). The psalmist gives the reason for this retelling in verses 9-11: "The men of Ephraim, though armed with bows, turned back on the day of battle; they did not keep God's covenant and refused to live by his law. They forgot what he had done, the wonders he had shown them."

Telling and retelling a story keeps it fresh in our minds. But the men of Ephraim forgot what God had done. As a result they "wimped out" in a crisis by acting as if God were not with them. Whenever the ancient Israelites forgot what God had done, their relationship with Him began to slip. So recounting the actions of God was not optional for them—it was a life-and-death matter as far as their relationship with Him was concerned. The good news is that whenever they started remembering and retelling God's stories, they returned to Him in practical ways as well.

"Shout with joy to God, all the earth! Sing the glory of his name; make his praise glorious! Say to God, 'How awesome are your deeds! So great is your power that your enemies cringe before you. All the earth bows down to you; they sing praise to you, they sing praise to your name.' Come and see what God has done, how awesome his works in man's behalf! He turned the sea into dry land, they passed through the waters on foot—come, let us rejoice in him" (Ps. 66:1-6).

Psalm 66 takes the idea of worship and recital one step further. The divine deeds it recited had powerfully changed history in a mighty way. Now by rehearsing a mighty act of God His people rekindled its power. As they recounted the deeds of God's past activities He became real to them in the present.

Such a concept of history has great inherent power. A clearly defined history provides people with a sense of identity and belonging. They know who they are and where they came from. And they know whom they belong to and whom they don't. We all need the belonging, the frame of reference, that comes when we know the history of our own family or of our own people. But more than this, the history of Israel became for them the foundation for worship, the basis for reminding each other what God had done for them. Without that history, their relationship with God was hit and miss. But through the retelling of that history they were able to rekindle the living presence of a mighty God.

CHAPTER 2

HOW IT ALL BEGAN

It's nice to have friends you can count on. Brooks is a card-carrying nut and a chronic practical joker. All the melancholy types run for cover when he approaches. But he is so much fun to be with that a crowd of children often surrounds him. He just fits right in. Whatever one may think of Brooks's sanguine ways, no friend of his will ever be in need. You can count on him.

When a youth group needs a driver for its bus, Brooks is quick to respond. If there is a weekend campout that requires adult supervision, he is there. Should your kids need a ride to some church activity, Brooks finds a way to pick them up. Or if you have to find a ride to the airport and don't know where to start, Brooks is willing to help. And the neat thing about it is that he responds with such generous eagerness that you don't ever feel guilty for asking. I really treasure people like him.

One of the most reassuring and powerful messages in the first part of the Bible is that God is a lot like my friend Brooks. He is consistent in His efforts to care for the needs around Him. You can count on Him, just as I have learned to count on Brooks. Let's take a closer look at this picture of God. We'll begin at the beginning.

THE CREATION STORY

The story about the origin of the human race starts in Genesis 1 and 2, the very first part of the Bible. The story of Creation opens a section that scholars call the primeval history, the first 11 chapters of Genesis. Genesis 1-11 is about the prehistoric period of earth's history, the period before our earliest firsthand records or archaeological evidence.

Within the Creation story, Genesis 1 gives you the big picture. It covers the entire Creation week—God's creation of slugs and eels, land and oceans, birds and mammals. The progression of the story through the original week leads up to the climax of the story, the creation of the first pair of human beings—the parents of the whole human race—Adam and Eve.

In Genesis 2, though, an interesting thing happens. The biblical author takes the rest of the creation for granted and zeroes in on the first couple. They become not only the center of attention, but virtually the sole focus of attention. The origin of the human race is the reason the author tells the story at all.

The key to the whole Creation story appears in Genesis 1:26-28. There God reveals His intention for the human race: "Then God said, 'Let us make man in our image, in our likeness, and let them rule over the fish of the sea and the birds of the air, over the livestock, over all the earth, and over all the creatures that move along the ground.' So God created man in his own image, in the image of God he created him; male and female he created them. God blessed them and said to them, 'Be fruitful and increase in number; fill the earth and subdue it. Rule over the fish of the sea and the birds of the air and over every living creature that moves on the ground.' "

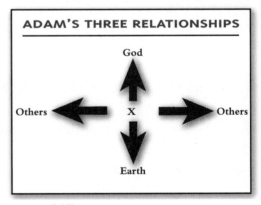

THREE BASIC RELATIONSHIPS

This text describes three basic relationships, illustrated above. Mr. X, in the center, is Adam. God created Adam in His image, making Him Adam's superior. Adam relates to God as his authority in a "mentor-client" or "mentor-disciple" type of relationship.

But while Genesis 1:26-28 strongly stresses the God-humanity dynamic, the text also emphasizes clearly that the image of God was both male and female. Adam and Eve are placed on a level of equality where they love and serve each other. This indicates that there is a social dimension to the image of God as well as a spiritual one.

But the image of God has a third dimension, a physical one. Not only do human beings have a relationship with God and a relationship with others, they also have a relationship with the earth. As stewards of the Creator, the human race is to cultivate the earth and make it a better place for all God's creatures to live. We see that relationship spelled out in more detail in Genesis 2, in which God expects Adam to care for the garden and gives him a position of authority over the animals.

THE FALL

So with Genesis 1 and 2 the human race gets off to a good start. The earth has peace, prosperity, and ordered relationships in a safe place. But it was not to last. Notice the stunning contrast between Genesis 1:27 and Genesis 6:5. First, "God created man in his own image, in the image of God he created him; male and female he created them" (Gen. 1:27). That sounds good, doesn't it? Everything's functioning the way it should. Then comes Genesis 6:5, only a short time after: "The Lord saw how great man's wickedness on the earth had become, and that every inclination of the thoughts of his heart was only evil all the time." The primeval history moves from "created in the image of God" to "every inclination of the thoughts of his heart was only evil all the time." What a difference and such a tragic change! What happened in the short time between these two passages? We call it "the Fall." The Fall shattered Eden's perfect relationships. And broken relationships are at the root of the world's evil.

This diagram looks a lot like the previous one, but this version illustrates that sin has two consequences: the natural consequences and the applied consequences. When our relationship with God gets broken, the natural consequence is fear—we become afraid of Him. And when our relationship with others shatters, the natural consequence is division, bickering, arguments, and violence. The fracturing of Adam's relationship with the earth had as its natural consequences decay and decline.

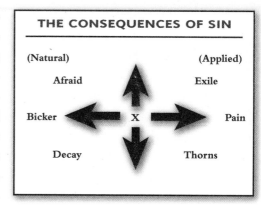

According to the biblical story, the natural consequences appear even before Adam and Eve again meet God. They become aware of their nakedness and take steps to remedy the situation (Gen. 3:7, 10, 11). God didn't make them fearful of Him—they experience fear even before He encounters them (verses 8-10). On the other hand, when God meets them face to face, He describes a further series of consequences (verses 16-19, 22-24). As sinners, Adam and Eve had to leave the garden and go into exile. No longer could they remain in God's direct presence. The pain of childbirth is another applied consequence of the broken relationships. And the complication of thorns and weeds in the environment added to the natural consequence of decay and death. What lies behind all of these "curses" is the ultimate individual penalty: death, eternal separation from God. The perspective of the Bible traces every aspect of the human tragedy to the Fall.

From Creation to Abraham
The Flood Story

The next big event after the Fall is the Flood narrative (Gen. 6-9). And this story is closely related to the one in Genesis 1-3. You see, in the creation of the physical earth, God had worked on the principle of separation and distinction. He separated the dry land from sea, and He separated the waters above from the waters below (Gen. 1:7, 9; cf. also verses 1:4, 18). The Flood story reverses that very same process. The waters from above come down and the waters from below rise up. The waters of the sea overwhelm the land, completely covering the earth and restoring the planet to its pre-Creation condition (Gen. 7:11, 20). The Flood story reverses the process of separation and distinction, undoing creation and returning the earth to pre-Creation chaos (Gen. 1:2, 9, 10; cf. 7:18-20).

But God doesn't leave things in chaos. After the Flood story He restores the earth by means of a new creation. The language of Genesis 8 and 9 picks up on that already used in Genesis 1 and 2 and 6 and 7. It expresses the rebuilding of creation. God repeats once again what He had done before. He begins with a wind over the watery chaos (Gen. 8:1; cf. 1:2). The vegetation returns (Gen. 8:11; cf. 1:12). God puts the animals back in their former environment (Gen. 8:17; cf. 1:25, 28) and reestablishes the seasons (Gen. 8:22; cf. 1:14-18). Once again He provides for the animals. Just as Adam took care of them in Eden, so Noah does it on the ark (Gen. 2:18-20; 7:6-10, 14-16). And the covenant God makes with Noah also echoes the language of Creation (cf. Gen. 1:28-30; 9:1-3).

DISCOVERING A PATTERN

What we see in these two stories sets the basis for a pattern. Because God works in a consistent fashion, His actions form their own patterns. Thus we find a consistency, a dependability, in His dealings that we do not observe in human actions. The only thing that we find dependable about human beings is their lack of consistency.

When you read broadly through the Old Testament you discover that it records four major divine acts. These four mighty deeds of God stand head and shoulders above all others. They are Creation, the Flood, the Exodus, and the Babylonian exile and return. We will see that a consistent pattern runs through them.

The Creation story of Genesis 1 and 2 begins with a situation of chaos: the waters cover the whole earth, and the Spirit or wind (it's the same word in the Hebrew) overshadows the waters. God divides the waters that are above from those that are below, allowing dry land to appear. Eventually He creates human beings in His image and gives them dominion over the earth. After He puts the man to sleep and forms the woman, they both live together in Paradise. The biblical account next speaks of the tree of life, a test involving the tree of the knowledge of good and evil, and a serpent.

As we have already seen, Scripture deliberately describes the destructive effects of the Flood in language reminiscent of Creation. The steps God took to build His creation in Genesis 1 and 2 He then reverses. He takes His creation apart in Genesis 6 and 7, and then He puts it back together again in Genesis 8 and 9. God follows a clear and consistent design or pattern, doing the same thing over again. On the other hand, He doesn't carry out

CREATION	FLOOD
Chaos	Chaos
Waters cover earth	Waters cover earth
Spirit overshadows	Wind blows
Waters divided	Ark
Dry land appears	Dry land appears
Image of God	
Dominion	Dominion
Put to sleep	
Woman formed	
Paradise	New earth
Tree of life	
Test	
Serpent	
Covenant implied	Covenant renewed

the whole pattern in every detail. So while God is consistent in His actions He is not mindless about it—His consistency is a creative one. He doesn't have to do everything He did before. While we observe a clear pattern in Genesis between the Flood and Creation, not every detail continues as the pattern unfolds. We will come back to this concept of pattern later on as we move through the Old Testament.

The Two Sides of Judgment

There is one other aspect of Genesis 4-11 that I would like to point out. God's judgments during the primeval history period were always twofold, both positive and negative. When people think of judgment, they often think of the negative. "Oh, no—they're going to check out all my personal record—I'm in big trouble!" But to the ancient Hebrews, judgment always had positive as well as negative aspects. We see this clearly after the Fall. God cursed the ground and banished Adam and Eve from the garden, certainly a negative consequence (Gen. 3:22-24). But on the positive side He makes clothing for them so they can handle the climate outside Paradise (verse 21). And He puts enmity between them and the serpent to limit its damage (verse 15). Even in their mistake, God judges them positively as well as negatively.

At first glance the story of Cain might also seem to be totally negative in its judgment. God offers Cain some choice words of rebuke (Gen. 4:6, 7) and banishes him from the human race (verses 11, 12). But divine judgment has a positive side as well. God puts a mark on Cain so that nobody will hurt him (verses 13-15). In the Flood story, of course, the negative judgment involves the destruction of the whole world and all the people in it. But on the positive side God provides the ark to set a group of people apart to carry on His mission.

Immediately after the Flood story we encounter the Tower of Babel. Again, the negative judgment is obvious—God confuses everyone's language and scatters the people (Gen. 11:7-9). The positive judgment is a lot less obvious, especially for Western minds with their chronological perspective. But if you read Genesis as a literary piece, Genesis 11 concludes with the story of Abraham. And what does God say to Abraham? "All peoples on earth will be blessed through you" (Gen. 12:3).

While our Western minds immediately note the gap of at least 600 years between Babel and Abraham, the language of the story line itself ties the call of Abraham back through the Tower of Babel story to the table of nations in Genesis 10. In that chapter you have a listing of all the nations of the world—it is the entire world in need of God, because it is a messed-up world that has fallen under the curse. Does God have a positive judgment for that world? Yes; it comes through Abraham.

Abraham as a Second Adam
A Threefold Promise

Genesis 12:1-3 declares: "The Lord had said to Abram, 'Leave your country, your people and your father's household and go to the land I will show you. I will make you into a great nation and I will bless you; I will make your name great, and you will be a blessing. I will bless those who bless you, and whoever curses you I will curse; and all peoples on earth will be blessed through you.'" A careful look at this passage shows that the promise to Abraham involves three things: God promises him a land, He promises that he will become a great nation, and He promises to make Abraham a blessing to others.

As you read your way through the Pentateuch—Genesis to Deuteronomy—you'll find some form of this threefold promise stated at least 25 times. The promise keeps getting repeated, reformulated, and restated in different ways. Let's take a look at just one of these restatements in Genesis 17, because it helps us to unpack the meaning of these three promises: the land, the nationhood, and the blessing. As you go through Genesis 17:1-8 below, look for hints of the three promises in it.

"When Abram was ninety-nine years old, the Lord appeared to him and said, 'I am God Almighty; walk before me and be blameless. I will confirm my covenant between me and you and will greatly increase your numbers.' Abram fell facedown, and God said to him, 'As for me, this is my covenant with you: You will be the father of many nations. . . . I will establish my covenant as an everlasting covenant between me and you and your descendants after you for the generations to come, to be your God and the God of your descendants after you. The whole land of Canaan, where you are now an alien, I will give as an everlasting possession to you and your descendants after you; and I will be their God.'"

First of all, Genesis 12 had the promise of blessing, but Genesis 17 now restates that promise. Instead of referring to blessing, God

THE PROMISES TO ABRAHAM	
Blessing Nation Land	Relationship Descendants Land (Canaan)

speaks of the covenant that He will establish with Abraham and with all of his descendants. Second, along with another allusion to nationhood, He talks about the numerous descendants Abraham will have. Third, God also restates the promise of the land and becomes more specific—it is to be the territory of Canaan.

ABRAHAM AND THE RESTORATION OF THE IMAGE OF GOD

Why does God promise Abraham these three things? Let's go back to the beginning for a moment. In the Creation story we noticed that the image of God involved the three basic relationships of Adam and Eve: to God, to each other, and to the earth. The original curse,

RELATIONSHIP	CURSE
God Others Earth	Exile Childbirth Thorns

then, specifically affected those three relationships: exile from the garden resulted from a break in the relationship between Adam and God; the childbirth pain affected the propagation of the human race and human relationships; and the thorns complicated the relationship between Adam and the earth. So the curse that comes in Genesis 3 in the Garden of Eden is a threefold one corresponding to the three relationships that made up the image of God that Adam and Eve received at the beginning.

Now let's take this a step further. In the original image of God the human race received a vertical relationship with God; God became our mentor, so to speak. But in Genesis 3 separation from God followed the Fall. Now in Genesis 12 and 17 comes a blessing—that full relationship with God would be restored in Abraham. The original image of God involved a harmonious union between the male and the female. After the Fall, however, this relationship came under the curse—symbolized by the pain of childbirth. In Genesis 12 and 17, however, God promises to restore human relationship through the nationhood of Abraham and his many descendants. The land, obviously, corresponds to both the original dominion in the garden and to the thorns that frustrated that dominion after the Fall.

So God promised Abraham not just a fresh start, but a restoration of Eden. He pledged to restore the fullness of the image of God. Not simply national in scope, the promises to Abraham signaled the full restoration of what the human race had lost in the Garden of Eden. The Tower of Babel represents the whole human race under the curse—the whole world in need of blessing. So when God calls Abraham, He does so with the rest of the human race in mind. He intends to restore the divine image and bring all peoples back to Paradise.

ABRAHAM: RESTORER OF CREATION

CREATION	CURSE	GEN. 12:1-3	GEN. 17:1-8
Image	Separation	Blessing	Relationship
Male and Female	Pain	Nation	Posterity
Dominion	Thorns	Land	Land

Of God's three promises to Abraham, the book of Genesis focuses mainly on the assurance of many descendants. You cannot populate a land without people. So at the climax of the book of Genesis comes the story of Joseph. The main point of the Joseph narrative appears in Genesis 46:3: "'I am God, the God of your father,' he said. 'Do not be afraid to go down to Egypt, for I will make you into a great nation there.'" Through the events recounted in the Joseph story God brought Abraham's descendants to a place that had plenty of food, so that it was possible for the people to multiply rapidly (Gen. 47:27).

Canaan had one drought after another. In Egypt, on the other hand, you didn't have to worry about the weather—it was sunny every day. Whenever you needed water, you could go to the Nile.

Egypt didn't have the agricultural problems that ancient Canaan had.

What happens because of a shortage of food? Children get sick and often don't make it to adulthood. Even today parents in some parts of the world have eight or nine children in the hope that, eventually, two or three will reach adulthood. God used Joseph to bring his family to Egypt so that they could be safe and grow according to the promise (Gen. 50:20). In Egypt a family of 70 (Ex. 1:5) would become a huge multitude.

THE STORY OF THE EXODUS

The Exodus is, in many ways, the focal point of the entire Old Testament. A mighty act of God, described on the same scale as the Creation or the Flood, it becomes a talking point for everything that follows in the Old Testament. Moving beyond that to the New Testament, the Exodus story provides many of the key New Testament terms for salvation, words such as "redeemed," "deliver," "ransom," "purchase," "slavery," and "freedom." So this story is a major piece of the Bible puzzle.

THE PROMISES FULFILLED		
GEN 12:1-3	GEN 17:1-8	PENTATEUCH
Blessing Nation Land	Relationship Posterity Land	Exodus/Leviticus Genesis Numbers/Deuteronomy

The four books that follow Genesis—Exodus, Leviticus, Numbers, and Deuteronomy—describe the Exodus event. These accounts pick up on the promises made to Abraham in Genesis 12 and 17. They show how the course of history fulfills the promises to Abraham. Genesis 12:1-3, then, is like the hinge of the Pentateuch. That central text first looks back on primeval history and focuses on dealing with the curse and restoration of the Garden of Eden. And then the promises God makes to Abraham set the tone for everything that follows. Genesis concentrates particularly on building up the population. (Moderns worry about overpopulation and have a hard time understanding the precariousness of human existence in the ancient world.) Exodus and Leviticus focus particularly on the promise of a renewed relationship with God. Numbers and Deuteronomy concentrate on the promise of land. So the Pentateuch is an intentional package put together to show the theological grounding of God's dealing with Israel.

Keeping in mind the chart on the previous page, let's take a brief look at the Exodus story. Just as the Flood consisted of an undoing and restoration of Creation, so the Exodus account also makes use of creation language. Exodus 14:21, 22 declares: "Then Moses stretched out his hand over the sea, and all that night the Lord drove the sea back with a strong east wind and turned it into dry land. The waters were divided, and the Israelites went through the sea on dry ground, with a wall of water on their right and on their left." Does the imagery of this text seem familiar? Again we find a chaotic sea acted upon by the wind (cf. Gen. 1:2; 8:1). Once more God divides the waters (cf. Gen. 1), producing dry ground. The author of Exodus 14 uses the specific terminology of Creation and the Flood to describe the mighty act of God by which Israel escaped from Egypt (this story is well known in popular culture through the blockbuster movies *The Ten Commandments* and *The Prince of Egypt*).

So the description of the Exodus clearly follows the pattern of Creation and the Flood. But now notice an interesting shift. No longer do the waters of chaos cover the entire earth. The story actually begins with "spiritual chaos"—the people are in slavery. Then the biblical writer describes the passage through the Red Sea in the language of both the Flood and the original creation. Scripture now replaces the dominion of Adam and Noah over the animals with the dominion over Canaan, the land of the promise. In place of the image of God, Scripture calls Israel God's "firstborn" (Ex. 4:22). So Israel becomes a second Adam, taking the place of Adam in the original creation. Whereas in Genesis God formed a woman shortly after the Creation, here He makes a people.

Taking the comparison further, the land of Canaan parallels the Paradise of the Garden of Eden. Whereas the garden had the tree of life, in the desert God's people had the manna to sustain them. Just as a serpent tested Adam and Eve in the garden, the Israelites were tested in the wilderness—the opposite of a garden—with a serpent. And, of course, the covenant came on Sinai.

THE PATTERN OF GOD'S SAVING ACTIONS

Now we can put together the big picture—the pattern of God's saving actions. Referring again to the chart below, we can see clearly a correlation between the three mighty acts of God: Creation, the Flood, and the Exodus. It again reminds us that God is consistent: when God acts, He does so in accordance with His character and with His own covenant. His earlier deeds become the model for His later ones.

THE PATTERN OF GOD'S SAVING ACTIONS		
CREATION	FLOOD	EXODUS
Chaos	Chaos	Spiritual chaos
Waters cover earth	Waters cover earth	Red Sea
Spirit overshadows	Wind blows	Wind blows
Waters divided	Ark	Waters divided
Dry land appears	Dry land appears	Dry land appears
Image of God		Firstborn
Dominion	Dominion	Dominion over Canaan
Put to sleep		
Woman formed		Creation of a people
Paradise	New earth	Canaan
Tree of life		Manna
Test		Test in wilderness
Serpent		Serpent
Covenant implied	Covenant renewed	Covenant

A careful look at the chart, however, shows that the sequence is not complete in every detail. God's consistency is not a mindless obsession. He is not like an autistic person who keeps doing or saying the same thing again and again. While that may be perfect consistency, it doesn't serve much of a practical purpose. God is not like that, nor is He bound to every detail of what He did before. While God's character and His covenant place certain limitations on His actions, He does not just blindly imitate His previous actions.

The Exodus displays a number of new features. For example, the birth of Moses and the threats he faced as a baby have no parallel in the Flood or Creation stories. But that experience of Moses sets a precedent for later deeds of God that we will address when we get there. So while God is consistent, He is not limited to previous patterns of action. Within an overall consistency, He can introduce new elements.

A further thing to note in this pattern is that the Exodus spiritualizes it. Water didn't actually cover the whole world this time, but spiritual chaos did, because God didn't have a people anywhere. He had called Abraham, yet the descendants of Abraham did not belong to Him. Pharaoh owned them. Spiritually speaking, the world was back to where it was before the Flood so that God had to perform a new creation all over again. So the pattern of His actions is not always literal—it can also be spiritual or figurative.

Now as we observe the pattern we have been examining, what language does the Bible employ to describe God's actions in a particular situation? It uses the language of the past. At every stage of Bible history the Bible writer has described God's activity in the present through the language or imagery of his past. When God speaks to Moses, he does so in the language of Moses' past—the language of the Creation and the Flood. The core of careful biblical interpretation demands that we respect the fact that God uses the language, culture, and experience of each biblical writer to get across the message He wanted to give.

So the Bible material comes in the time, place, language, and circumstance of the original writer. If you want to understand the Pentateuch, you've got to start where Moses was. Should you want to understand Daniel, you have to know something of what life was like back then. Or if you want to understand Revelation or Romans, you have to "get under the skin" of the New Testament author. You have to grasp each writer's world—his or her language, time, and place. God meets people where they are.

Conclusion

Not too long ago anyone reading the Old Testament for the first time in a Western country found it to be very strange. The behavior of the people and even that of God was very foreign to Western ways of thinking (sometimes called modernism today). Reading the Bible in a Western context raised more questions than it answered, and many people lost their faith.

At the same time many people in the developing countries were still living in a world not that much different from that of the Old Testament. Their life experience and thinking patterns continued in many ways to parallel the Hebrew culture of the Bible. So they often found (and still find) the Bible easier to appreciate than Westerners do. But today the situation has changed in Western countries. Secular Westerners are increasingly seeing the world in ways similar to Old Testament times. We sometimes call this more Hebraic style of thinking postmodernism. But while the younger generation is more likely to think like people did in Bible times, a living experience with Jesus is, in most cases, still to come for them.

A main reason Christian faith has so little impact on the world today is that most Christians read the Bible in Greek Western terms that are both inappropriate to the scriptural material and increasingly incomprehensible to the average person on the street, whether in Boston or Bombay, Berlin or Bujumbura. That is the reason I wrote this book. When we explore the full impact of Hebrew thinking, the Bible again becomes a life-changing book.

CHAPTER 3

ISRAEL AS A NATION

Histories of the twentieth century read like one giant experiment in government. A large portion of the Eurasian land mass experimented with Communism, in theory placing government in the hands of the working classes, who in most places had generally found themselves excluded from any significant influence on world affairs. Other countries explored extreme forms of nationalism ("my country, right or wrong") such as the Nazism of Germany and the Fascism of Italy. Countries such as Sweden opted for kinder, gentler versions of socialism, in which the government took upon itself cradle-to-grave responsibility for all of its citizens. More recently has come a wave of American-style democratic capitalism, dedicated to the idea that free trade and the entrepreneurial spirit provide the best quality of life for the most people. Finally, we should mention China's attempt to combine the best characteristics of Communism and capitalism into an unlikely blend of economic freedom and political repression that seems to be working fairly well at the moment.

Each political experiment had its pros and cons. The advantages of Communism, for example, include a high degree of security for the average person. The government assures jobs and health care for everyone. Crime is low and gets severely punished whenever it occurs. Life from cradle to grave is fairly predictable, and this is quite attractive to many (witnessed by the unhappiness of many East Germans who suddenly found themselves dragged into the vigorous uncertainty of democratic capitalism by the unification of 1990).

In practice, however, Communism resulted in the sacrifice of much freedom, which many human beings consider basic to any quality of life. Communism also proved to be an extremely inefficient way to do business, and produced a horrific record with regard to the environment. Although attempting to be a government "of the people," in practice it was nearly always abusive and unfair, the leaders being rewarded with privileges and power, the people as a whole losing the right to self-determination and self-improvement.

As an American, I must confess that democratic capitalism has its pros and cons as well. On the positive side, my form of government has certainly encouraged the greatest and broadest surge of prosperity in the world's history. Americans are free to be what they want to be, do what they want to do (within a few limits), and go where they want to go. Democratic capitalism promotes personal advancement and great progress in science and technology. Every person has the opportunity to achieve a high level of self-actualization.

Democratic capitalism, on the other hand, offers a fairly low level of personal security. Its social safety net is full of cracks and holes that people fall through. Also, it has exhibited a strong tendency to discriminate against minorities (the tyranny of the majority) and to exploit the environment for short-term profit. Day trading and hedge funds have encouraged companies to pursue the short-term fix rather than take the long view of what might be best. And finally, democracy tends to produce inertia over time as the checks and balances of American government often result in governmental gridlock, making meaningful change extremely hard to accomplish.

So if there is one thing that we have learned from the governmental experiments of the past century, it is that our world has no ideal form of government. Each has its advantages and disadvantages. Most systems of government look better from a distance (in a country I visited recently, nearly everyone I talked to dreamed of one day moving to America). Ancient Israel discovered this lesson the hard way. As it settled into the Promised Land it had a unique form of government in which God ruled directly through personal representatives such as Moses and Joshua. "Elders" and a stair-step system that filtered leadership down from rulers of "ten thousands" (the 12 tribes) to rulers of thousands, hundreds, and tens assisted the great national leaders. But it was not long before Israelites began to think that Egypt and Babylon had a better idea.

THE DEUTERONOMIC HISTORY

With the book of Joshua we move from the Exodus to Israel's settled experience in the Promised Land. So if you start from the book of Genesis and work your way through the Pentateuch to the books of Joshua, Judges, Samuel, and Kings, you'll find that they form one connected history, a single continuing narrative. It is as if a single individual sat down and wrote the entire story.

The book of Deuteronomy provides the transition between the setting of the Exodus and the settled history in Canaan that followed. The term *deuteronomy* means "second law." What was the first law? The law given at Sinai and recorded in Exodus and Leviticus (and part of Numbers). The purpose of the first law was to regulate Israel's relationship with God in the desert. Deuteronomy, on the other hand, was not a law for the desert, but a constitution for when God's people occupied the land. So the book of Deuteronomy provides a natural bridge between the Exodus and the history that follows in Canaan.

A number of scholars have seen the unity of the picture running from Genesis through 2 Kings and come up with the term *Deuteronomic history*. From Joshua through 2 Kings Scripture assesses the subsequent history of Israel in light of the book of Deuteronomy. The biblical writers judge history by the laws of Deuteronomy. When a king does the right thing according to Deuteronomy, then Scripture considers him a good king, but when he ignores the law, or does evil, then it regards him as an evil king.

Why would anybody write such histories? Most historians write history to influence the time in which they live. Histories help us learn from the mistakes of the past. The biblical histories, therefore, are like a call to repentance for those reading at a later time. While

Israel's histories are about God's mighty deeds, they also record the actions of His people. And it's a pretty ugly account much of the time. They are consistently unfaithful, constantly stumbling, continually getting into trouble. But such histories are valuable because they help us learn from the mistakes of others.

One thing I see about Scripture is that it allows us to benefit from the mistakes and failures of its characters. We see the Israelites repeating the mistakes of Adam again and again. When Israel rehearsed its history, the people not only confirmed their understanding of God, they gained a better understanding of themselves as well. It was as if the Bible presented two parallel principles: God was always faithful, and His people were always unfaithful. In a sense both Israel and God were equally consistent—you could almost predict what both were going to do.

And here's the interesting thing. We saw in the previous chapter that God's purpose through Abraham was to restore the Garden of Eden. And that's what the land of Canaan represented. But as you go through the entire Old Testament, what do you discover? The restoration of Eden never happened.

What does that say about the Old Testament? That it's an unfinished book. No religion based solely on the Old Testament could be a complete religion. What about Judaism? you ask. Judaism is not a religion of the Old Testament. Rather it is a religion that interprets and expands on the Old Testament. In writings such as the Mishnah and the Talmud we see an oral tradition that paralleled the Old Testament and interacted with it. Christianity, of course, has its New Testament and employs the same foundation. Islam, which also shares the Old Testament heritage, has the Koran. So you have basically three ways by which the Old Testament can become a living, practical faith in today's world.

Which of these three traditions builds most closely on the Old Testament? I would like to suggest that the best way to expand on the Old Testament would be the way that it naturally interprets itself. In this book you will see how the Old Testament material develops ideas in relationship to itself and then observe how the New Testament takes up the same path of interpretation, handling the Old Testament with deep respect. This is vital for a Christian understanding of the Bible.

In any case, we can summarize this section by noting that the Deuteronomic history examines whether Israel has kept its covenant with God, usually coming to a fairly negative conclusion. The purpose of this section of Scripture is to call its readers to repentance—a total commitment to God. We will now turn to the two major periods of Israel's settlement in Canaan that form the heart of the accounts in the Deuteronomic history.

THE HISTORY OF THE LAND: A PERIOD OF ANARCHY

When Israel first settled in the Promised Land, the people had no strong central government. Instead they experienced a period of scattered local control. Judges 17:6 summarizes it this way: "In those days Israel had no king; everyone did as he saw fit." Instead of a strong central government we find frequent chaos, a sense of everyone for themselves. The story in the book of Judges actually describes cycles of chaos or, to put it another way, an extended period of anarchy.

During this time of social and religious breakdown the 12 tribes experienced a number of minor "rehearsals" or reenactments of the Exodus, if you will. God again and again repeated, on a smaller scale, His mighty act of bringing Israel out of Egypt. On at least 12 different occasions in the book of Judges a portion of the Israelites became captive to an outside power for a time, then God would send a "judge" to deliver them, just as He had called Moses to deliver all the tribes out of Egypt. The most famous of the 12 judges were Gideon and Samson.

Reading Judges reminds me of what Yogi Berra once said: "It's déjà vu all over again." The cycle of disaster and rescue kept repeating itself. Who was faithful during this period? God was. He was always there, always bringing in a judge, or savior, when the

Israelites needed one. The people, on the other hand, were consistently unfaithful. After several hundred years it became evident that chaos as a method of government was not working. It didn't provide a sufficient element of security for daily life. So by the time of 1 Samuel a groundswell among the people began to demand, "We need a more centralized leadership; we need something more like what the other nations have—we need a king."

THE HISTORY OF THE LAND: THE ROLE OF THE MONARCHY

But that did not turn out to be the total answer either. Monarchy would bring in its own set of problems. The books of Samuel address the issue of kingship. In fact, Samuel the prophet makes several speeches about it. Let's look at one of the shorter ones, found in 1 Samuel 10:17-25. As you read it, ask yourself the question "Was kingship God's will or not?"

First Samuel 10:17, 18: "Samuel summoned the people of Israel to the Lord at Mizpah and said to them, 'This is what the Lord, the God of Israel, says: "I brought Israel up out of Egypt, and I delivered you from the power of Egypt and all the kingdoms that oppressed you."'" What was Samuel doing here? He was recounting the history of Israel—rehearsing the mighty acts of God. This is, as we have seen, a continuous practice throughout the Old Testament. But after reciting God's powerful deeds, he then presents the other side of the coin:

"But you have now rejected your God, who saves you out of all your calamities and distresses. And you have said, 'No, set a king over us.' So now present yourselves before the Lord by your tribes and clans" (verse 19). Here's an interesting point: Israel is the product of a history in which God has intervened mightily for them, but at the same time, Israel has consistently rejected what He did for them.

According to 1 Samuel 10:19, was Israelite kingship God's will or not? The answer would seem to be no. The way the book of Judges portrays the anarchy, it seems to be calling for a king. But the two perspectives do not contradict each other when you look at the whole context of Samuel's speech.

"When Samuel brought all the tribes of Israel near, the tribe of Benjamin was chosen. Then he brought forward the tribe of Benjamin, clan by clan, and Matri's clan was chosen. Finally Saul son of Kish was chosen. But when they looked for him, he was not to be found. So they inquired further of the Lord, 'Has the man come here yet?'

"And the Lord said, 'Yes, he has hidden himself among the baggage.'

"They ran and brought him out, and as he stood among the people he was a head taller than any of the others. Samuel said to all the people, 'Do you see the man the Lord has chosen? There is no one like him among all the people.'

"Then the people shouted, 'Long live the king!'

"Samuel explained to the people the regulations of the kingship. He wrote them down on a scroll and deposited it before the Lord. Then Samuel dismissed the people, each to his own home" (verses 20-25).

All other things being equal, it would have been better to have God as a king than any human being. But as the book of Judges makes clear, things in this life are not always equal. So God adopts the concept of kingship in spite of its flaws. In one sense, the way the people asked, as well as their purpose, constituted a rejection of God and His agent Samuel. At the same time, though, God adopts the idea and instructs them how to make it work. And He chooses who the leader will be.

This raises an interesting question about God. Why does He accept and even take over an institution that He believes to be negative for His people? Does He feel that it is the best thing for them in that particular situation? Or is He letting them have their way, as parents sometimes do, in the hopes that they might learn something? The problem with kingship in the light of Deuteronomy (and Deuteronomy anticipates that they will one day ask for a king—Deuteronomy 17:14-20) is that now a king represents Israel before God. And the behavior of that king, in a sense, stands for the whole people. The people have shifted their corporate responsibility before God to a single person, who will act in their behalf. The Deuteronomic covenant blesses or curses the nation's obedience or disobedience. Now, suddenly, one person has the power to undo the whole thing.

If that one person decides to be evil, the whole nation suffers. Daniel (Dan. 9:1-19) and many godly Israelites went into exile as a result of the mistakes of one king after another. Because the kings were consistently evil throughout much of Israel and Judah's history, the entire nation slid into a downhill spiral that ended up in captivity. And throughout this history, the conflict between God and Israel became a struggle between prophet and king. The prophet speaks for God, the king for the people, and the interaction between the two becomes the essence of the matter. Because Israel gave up its responsibility and turned it over to a king, the interaction between God and His people now becomes the interaction of prophet and king.

In a sense, the new situation split roles. Under the judges, both prophet and king were the same person. The prophet, so to speak, acted as king, creating unity of action between God and His representative. But when the new circumstances separated the two roles, too often only the prophet was listening to God and the king was simply acting as a politician. Thus most of the time things did not go well.

During this period, though, God continued to deliver His people from the various captivities they got themselves into. We see these mini-acts of God in the repeated battles between the Philistines and the Israelites. At various times Samson, Saul, and finally David led the Israelites. Then came conflict between Rehoboam and the Egyptians. Later we find stories of Israel struggling with Assyria and Syria, and Judah fought Moab, Ammon, Assyria, and Babylon. Again and again throughout this history you have God being faithful and the people being consistently unfaithful. We will now turn to the situation of the later prophets of the Old Testament. These puzzling books have one great central theme.

CHAPTER 4

EXILE AND RETURN

As I was nearing the end of my college years, my thoughts turned quite seriously toward the issue of a life partner. I had met many girls, and from time to time thought that maybe this or that one might be the *one*. But things never quite worked out. I sort of figured that college was the best possibility and the maximum opportunity for selection. So as I entered my senior year I began to get a little anxious about it.

After some thought and a lot of prayer, I decided to leave the matter in God's hands. After all, who was in a better position to match me up with the right person than the Creator of everybody? I sat back and envisioned a delightful future with the ideal person of God's choosing.

Not long after that it happened! A casual date with someone I had never particularly noticed before completely changed my world. We seemed to have every interest in common, and found each other's every comment fascinating and every joke uproariously funny. On top of that, whenever we moved away from the fun stuff to serious talk, everything pointed to as close an ideal match as either of us could have imagined. I couldn't believe that God could make such a great selection—and so quickly!

A few things needed to be cleared up before we could do any long-range planning, so she made a trip back to her home country to deal with those matters and make sure that her family would support the new direction she was going. I spent the weeks that she was away praising God, dreaming, role playing, and preparing myself for the hard work of relationship building that lay ahead.

The future looked bright under God's guidance and blessing.

One small problem developed, though. Well, I guess it was a pretty big problem. She never came back! After a week or two in her home country she began to see things in a different light. She decided to move her life in another direction. A tear-stained letter explained what was happening and wished me well.

As you can imagine, I was pretty angry with God about the whole thing. Here I had trusted Him to do what was best for me and what did He do? He had dangled an ideal before me and then snatched it away just as I was getting used to it. God gave me the realization of my dreams and then smashed it before my eyes. Naturally, at that point I didn't think very much of the way He fulfills His promises. I had my doubts as to whether God really knew what He was doing in the matter of romance. At the time I didn't grasp how similar my experience was to that of Israel, as described in the Old Testament prophets.

GOD'S FOURTH GREAT MIGHTY ACT

In chapter 2 we spent some time walking through Creation, the Flood, and the Exodus story, and saw the clear patterns in God's saving actions. We noticed that God is consistent but doesn't necessarily repeat every detail of His prior action. He can do new things within an overall harmony. While His deeds display a definite pattern, He still sometimes surprises us.

In this chapter we turn to God's fourth great mighty act in the Old Testament: the exile to Babylon and the return after 70 years. This single event is the main theme of the Old Testament prophets from Isaiah to Malachi. Some of the prophets preached before the Exile and predicted it, including Hosea, Amos, and Isaiah. Others wrote during the Exile, such as Daniel and Ezekiel. Still others served afterward, such as Malachi and Zechariah. So the major point of interest in the prophets was this great event that was coming or, in some cases, had already happened.

Now let's put together some things we learned in the second

chapter. There we saw that Scripture describes each mighty act of God with the language of His previous deeds. So when the prophets start writing about the exile to Babylon, what language would you expect them to use? The language of their past. What is the past of Isaiah? of Jeremiah? And of Hosea and Amos? It is God's mighty act for Israel in the Exodus. If the pattern remains consistent, we should expect that God will portray the exile from Babylon in the phraseology of His previous mighty acts—particularly the Exodus.

HOSEA

Let's start with Hosea 2:8-15. A prophet who looked forward toward the Exile, Hosea wrote somewhere around 760 B.C. (The Exile occurred partially about 722 B.C. and completely about 586 B.C.) In Hosea 2:8 God says with reference to Israel: "She has not acknowledged that I was the one who gave her the grain, the new wine and oil, who lavished on her the silver and gold—which they used for Baal." Notice the fascinating dynamic of this verse. God is rehearsing His previous mighty actions for them. Not just the Exodus, not just something way, way back, but He declares, "Hey, look at your new wine, oil, grain, gold, silver. Everything you have, you got from Me." What was Israel's problem? They did not acknowledge what God had done for them—they did not rehearse His mighty acts. The people did not remind themselves continually that it was God who had done these things in their experience.

A little background to the text will help us understand it better. At this point in time, Israel is under the rulership of Jereboam II. He's a king that the Old Testament does not have much to say about, but we do know that his reign was an incredibly prosperous time. Jereboam II ruled over a territory nearly as large as that of David. Apparently the superpowers of the time, Egypt and Assyria, were both struggling economically and politically. With them out of the way, Israel became a mini superpower in its own right for a few years. So you would think, after all the hard times they'd been through, that they'd be thankful to God for the good times. But it was not so. According to Hosea 2:8, they forgot the source of their good things and instead praised Baal.

In verse 9 God told them, "Therefore I will take away my grain when it ripens, and my new wine when it is ready. I will take back my wool and my linen, intended to cover her nakedness." Do you hear an echo of Deuteronomy 28 here? Depending on how they respond to His mighty acts, either prosperity will come or difficult times will overwhelm them. Verses 10-13 of Hosea 2 announce: "'So now I will expose her lewdness before the eyes of her lovers; no one will take her out of my hands. I will stop all her celebrations: her yearly festivals, her New Moons, her Sabbath days—all her appointed feasts. I will ruin her vines and her fig trees, which she said were her pay from her lovers; I will make them a thicket, and wild animals will devour them. I will punish her for the days she burned incense to the Baals; she decked herself with rings and jewelry, and went after her lovers, but me she forgot,' declares the Lord."

Do you see what Israel's problem was? Its focus was not on what God had done, but on what it had gained. They imagined the Lord to be like a vending machine from which you get whatever you want when you want it. But people don't think a lot about vending machines between snacks, do they? This is animistic thinking: manipulating the gods to keep the rain and the prosperity coming. The Canaanite god Baal was the god of thunder and storm. So he was the deity that provided rain. And the people of the Bible lived in a part of the world that never has enough rain. So if you could get Baal to bring more rain, everything would be great.

Thus Israel failed to put God first in the midst of its prosperity. Instead it fell back into primitive ways of relating to God. But notice verse 14, in which God steps in to help them anyway: "Therefore I am now going to allure her; I will lead her into the desert and speak tenderly to her." What's the desert allusion all about? It is a subtle reminder of Israel's experience during the Exodus. God is bringing to their memory the mighty actions He had done for them in the past. Israel forgets to remind themselves what God has done, so He does it for them. It's a pattern we observe throughout the Old Testament—when Israel stops rehearsing, God rehearses for them.

Here God offers a solution. He says, "I'm going to bring her back into the desert. I'm going to do the Exodus all over again." It's like a love story. God looks back on Israel's youth, when the nation was young. He and Israel were dating—so to speak—in the desert. In later years the marriage has gotten rough and God is thinking about divorcing her, but instead He comes up with a plan. "Let's go back and do the things that got us together in the first place! Let's start dating again!"

Notice verse 15: "There [in the desert] I will give her back her vineyards, and will make the Valley of Achor a door of hope. There she will sing as in the days of her youth, as in the day she came up out of Egypt." Here we have the incredible story of a God who has lost His lover. No longer does she think about Him. Instead, she obsesses about other gods all the time.

So in this passage God develops a twofold strategy to win her back. First, she must discover what life would be like without Him. She has to lose the vending machine and in the process hit bottom. People have to hit bottom before they are willing to do whatever it takes to gain a better life. Some people refer to what God did here as "tough love." Others describe it by the term *intervention*. Whatever you call it, it's a constant theme in the prophets. And in the dark times, when everything falls apart, God returns and tries to allure Israel back to Himself. If she does return to Him, then the suffering will be worth it all even though He would rather make her prosperous. So God's tough-love plan for Israel is a new wilderness experience. And what does that new wilderness experience consist of? The Exile, described in terms of a new Exodus. God's goal in putting Israel into exile is to lure her back to Himself.

Micah

Let's move on to Micah, who prophesied in Judah about 750 B.C. He offers a message similar to Hosea's. Micah 7:15-20: "'As in the days when you came out of Egypt, I will show them my wonders.' Nations will see and be ashamed, deprived of all their power. They will lay their hands on their mouths and their ears will become deaf. . . . Who is a God like you, who pardons sin and forgives the transgression of the remnant of his inheritance? You do not stay angry forever but delight to show mercy. You will again have compassion on us; you will tread our sins underfoot and hurl all our iniquities into the depths of the sea. You will be true to Jacob, and show mercy to Abraham, as you pledged on oath to our fathers in days long ago."

Notice that once again a prophet addresses the Exile from the perspective of the Exodus. He refers to "wonders" in the land of Egypt and the promises made to Abraham. But the point of emphasis in Micah is not Israel's physical move into exile and their physical return after 70 years. Instead, the biblical writer has in view here the spiritual nature of such a pilgrimage. The "exodus" from Babylon will involve pardon, forgiveness, mercy, and compassion. Israel's consistent unfaithfulness will be forgotten like something that falls to the bottom of the sea, something the Egyptian armies had done a thousand years before.

So once again we find a spiritualization of the type. The real enemy is no longer the Egyptians or the Babylonians, but the sins and failures of God's own people. Their captivity to sin and unproductive behavior is as much in view as their physical captivity to any particular foreign nation. The exile, from God's perspective, is not so much a political or economic issue as it is a spiritual one.

Isaiah

But release from exile has a physical aspect as well. Let's look at another prophet, this one named Isaiah. He had a lot of things to say about the Exile even before it happened. Isaiah 11:15: "The Lord will dry up the gulf of the Egyptian sea; with a scorching wind he will sweep his hand over the Euphrates River." What the prophet is doing here is speaking of a future event in the language of the past.

He compares the Red Sea experience (in Egypt) with Israel's future experience by the Euphrates River (the river of Babylon). Isaiah 11:15, 16 continues: "He will break it [the Euphrates River] up into seven streams so that men can cross over in sandals. There will be a highway for the remnant of his people that is left from Assyria, as there was for Israel when they came up from Egypt."

Isaiah is saying, "Like the Red Sea experience, God will deliver again. But this time it will be the Euphrates River. This time it will not involve Egypt but Assyria." He describes a future event in the imagery and phraseology of the past. When they go into exile, the pattern of Israel's experience in Egypt will be instructive for Israel.

Let us consider another text from Isaiah—Isaiah 43:16, 17: "This is what the Lord says—he who made a way through the sea, a path through the mighty waters, who drew out the chariots and horses, the army and reinforcements together, and they lay there, never to rise again, extinguished, snuffed out like a wick." Here we find the language of the Exodus again. In verses 18 and 19, however, the prophet makes an interesting switch. "Forget the former things; do not dwell on the past. See, I am doing a new thing! Now it springs up; do you not perceive it? I am making a way in the desert and streams in the wasteland." What's the message of this text? It's telling us that the future will be *like* the past but not *limited* to it. The past provides the language of the future, but the future itself will transcend the past.

In fact, God gets so excited about what He's going to do during and after the exile to Babylon that the language of the Exodus is no longer adequate. It forces Him all the way back to Creation to find imagery big enough to describe the mighty act that He has in mind. Isaiah 65:17-19: "Behold, I will create new heavens and a new earth. The former things will not be remembered, nor will they come to mind. But be glad and rejoice forever in what I will create, for I will create Jerusalem to be a delight and its people a joy. I will rejoice over Jerusalem and take delight in my people; the sound of weeping and of crying will be heard in it no more."

This is a favorite text of those who would like to understand the life of heaven better. But notice what happens in verse 20: "Never again will there be in it an infant who lives but a few days, or an old man who does not live out his years; he who dies at a hundred will be thought a mere youth; he who fails to reach a hundred will be considered accursed." I thought dying wasn't supposed to occur in heaven? True (Rev. 20:14; 21:4). But remember that this passage appears in the context of Israel's return from exile. As with the covenant promises of Deuteronomy, the restoration of the land and the people was to be gradual. Their obedience to God would enable Him to do greater and greater things for them until the land of Canaan became the Garden of Eden all over again. The Old Testament expectation did not have the kind of sudden change represented by the New Testament concept of the second coming of Jesus.

From Prophecy to Fulfillment

With prophets such as Haggai and Zechariah we come to the time of fulfillment, the period after the Exile. But the reality of fulfillment was quite a bit different than a reading of the prophets might have led us to assume. From them we might have expected millions of people streaming back from exile when in reality it was only 50,000. And instead of great miracles as at the time of the Exodus the return involved just a lot of hard work.

It's no wonder that in reading the postexilic prophets you discover that God's people became discouraged. Israel was still suffering persecution—Persia was still in control. It became increasingly clear that it was not the best that God could do. The great, final deliverance was yet to come.

So the Old Testament closes with a fulfillment of the prophecies about the Exile. But it's a disappointing one. That is why no one has ever built a religion solely on the Old Testament. Incomplete in itself, it cries out for completion. The three great religions based on the Old Testament all have a supplement of some kind: a Talmud, a Koran, or a New Testament.

Thus you can't base a complete faith on the Old Testament alone. The Old Testament simply roots us in the reality of where we are and in the hopelessness of that reality. It points us to an incredible mighty act of God that is yet to come. And that sets the table for the New Testament, which we will turn to in the next chapter. But first, let's look at a couple of postexilic texts to get a sense of how things appeared at the end of the Old Testament period.

Haggai 2:1-3: "On the twenty-first day of the seventh month, the word of the Lord came through the prophet Haggai: 'Speak to Zerubbabel son of Shealtiel, governor of Judah, to Joshua son of Jehozadak, the high priest, and to the remnant of the people. Ask them, "Who of you is left who saw this house in its former glory? How does it look to you now? Does it not seem to you like nothing?"'" God recognizes that to them, this isn't the real fulfillment. Things have not been transformed in the way that they expected.

Verses 4, 5: "'But now be strong, O Zerubbabel,' declares the Lord. 'Be strong, O Joshua son of Jehozadak, the high priest. Be strong, all you people of the land,' declares the Lord, 'and work. For I am with you,' declares the Lord Almighty. 'This is what I covenanted with you when you came out of Egypt. And my Spirit remains among you. Do not fear.'" Was this the fulfillment? Yes, it was. But it was a disappointing culmination for them. They had read the prophecies, and they were looking for more. But that is not all that God has to say.

Verses 6-9: "This is what the Lord Almighty says: 'In a little while I will once more shake the heavens and the earth, the sea and the dry land. I will shake all nations, and the desired of all nations will come, and I will fill this house with glory,' says the Lord Almighty. 'The silver is mine and the gold is mine,' declares the Lord Almighty. 'The glory of this present house will be greater than the glory of the former house,' says the Lord Almighty. 'And in this place I will grant peace,' declares the Lord Almighty."

At the close of the Old Testament God assures His people, "Everything is on track. My greatest, mightiest act hasn't happened yet, but don't get discouraged; everything's on course. I haven't lost control of the situation here." His hand will yet accomplish a great and mighty future shaking.

Zechariah 9:9, 10 puts another spin on the same future: "Rejoice greatly, O Daughter of Zion! Shout, Daughter of Jerusalem! See, your king comes to you, righteous and having salvation, gentle and riding on a donkey, on a colt, the foal of a donkey. I will take away the chariots from Ephraim and the war-horses from Jerusalem, and the battle bow will be broken. He will proclaim peace to the nations. His rule will extend from sea to sea and from the River to the ends of the earth."

Now I ask you, can you blame many of the Jews for thinking that the Messiah would be a little bit more glorious than Jesus seemed to be? It's easy to misunderstand a prophecy before its time. But what they missed—and it's easy to overlook—is the spiritual aspect of the promise. With the spiritualizing of the type you find as you move through the Old Testament, the fulfillment more and more came to the eyes of faith only. The fulfillment in Haggai was through the eyes of faith. But to the eyes of sight, it was a disappointment. Yet God said to them, "This is the fulfillment." So when you come to the end of the Old Testament, you may find yourself tempted to cry out, "This couldn't be the best that God can do!" And you would be right. The best that God could do is waiting for us in the New Testament.

In my own disappointment back in my senior year of college I too had a sense that my abortive relationship was not the best that God could do. Through my tears and through my doubts, I hung on to the concept that God was in control of things and that it would all work out for the best in the end. But though I believed God in my mind, my heart didn't feel it. I didn't know that the love of my life was waiting just around the corner, someone I had never met in all my years of college. At the end of my "Old Testament" experience it was hard to imagine that something even greater lay just ahead. I didn't know then that God would wait until one week after graduation to introduce me to His final fulfillment of my request. This much I can assure you—God's best is always worth waiting for!

CHAPTER 5

THE PATTERN OF NEW TESTAMENT FAITH

The New Testament did not get written in a vacuum, but builds on the Old Testament and its stories about Adam, Abraham, and Israel. It applies the whole history and experience of the Old Testament saints to Jesus, using the method of typology, or spiritualization of the type, a method we have already seen illustrated in the Old Testament. Thus the New Testament interprets the Old the same way that the Old interprets itself.

In each section of this chapter we will offer clear, unambiguous texts that demonstrate the New Testament association of Jesus with a specific Old Testament character or historical situation. We will then examine His life and experience to show how the New Testament writers might have made such an association. We will find that they based almost everything Jesus said and did on the words and actions of Old Testament predecessors. Jesus is the fulfillment and the natural successor of Adam, Isaac, Moses, Israel, David, Solomon, and Elisha, to name just a few. To ignore the parallels is to misunderstand what Jesus meant to them. And if we fail to grasp the significance Jesus had for them, there is a good chance that we will not understand what He means to us either.

THE NEW CREATION

The Old Testament clearly anticipates that God would one day create new heavens and a new earth (Isa. 65:17) in the context of a restored Jerusalem (verses 18-20). In the New Testament, however, the expectation undergoes a surprising transformation. The concept of the new creation finds its fulfillment in the person and the work of Jesus Christ, when He appeared on earth some 2,000 years ago.

We begin our look at the New Testament use of Old Testament history with the first verse of the Gospel of John: "In the beginning was the Word, and the Word was with God, and the Word was God" (John 1:1). It is significant that the first words of the Greek translation of the Old Testament are "in the beginning God made the heaven and the earth" (Gen. 1:1). The Gospel of John and the book of Genesis both open with the same phrase: "in the beginning." But in the place of God creating heaven and the earth, John simply states: "in the beginning was the Word" (a title for Jesus in the book—cf. John 1:14). The apostle sees Jesus as in some sense the full equivalent of the original creation. When Jesus came to this earth, God was doing a new creation. Jesus as *the Word* corresponds to "and God said."

We find this idea repeated many times in various ways in the New Testament. Notice Luke 1:35: "The angel answered, 'The Holy Spirit will come upon you, and the power of the Most High will overshadow you. So the holy one to be born will be called the Son of God.'" The Greek phrase translated "overshadow" here reminds us of the Spirit of God moving upon the waters of the original creation in Genesis 1:2. When the Spirit overshadowed the waters of the earth, the result was the original creation. Then when the Spirit overshadowed Mary it led to the conception and the birth of Jesus. Once again, we need to understand Jesus as God's new creation.

Twice the apostle Paul draws a strong analogy between Adam and Jesus. Romans 5 depicts Jesus as a new Adam who undoes the consequences that Adam's original sin had for the entire human race (verses 12-19). By Jesus' mighty act of righteousness He brings life to a human race subject to Adam's sentence of death. First Corinthians 15 makes a similar point: "For as in Adam all die, so in Christ all will be made alive" (verse 22). Here Jesus is the "Last Adam," or the "Second Adam," who comes from heaven and provides the possibility for human beings to overcome death through the resurrection at the "last trumpet" (verses 45-57). So for Paul Jesus is not only the new creation, He is the ideal counterpart of the original Adam as well.

We see this further underlined when New Testament writers use the "image of God" concept in relation to Jesus. Adam was the original embodiment of the divine image. Now God restores it in the person of Jesus. "He is the image of the invisible God, the firstborn over all creation" (Col. 1:15). "The god of this age has blinded the minds of unbelievers, so that they cannot see the light of the gospel of the glory of Christ, who is the image of God" (2 Cor. 4:4; cf. Heb. 1:3).

In what sense is Jesus the new Adam? Jesus is like Adam in all of His relationships. As with the original Adam Jesus had a perfect relationship with God, with others, and with the environment around Him. He came to earth to become what God intended Adam to be.

Jesus in John 14:28 comments that "the Father is greater than I." As the new Adam, Jesus was in perfect subordination to His Father. And as the image of God He obeyed His Father's commands (John 15:10). Thus as the Second Adam Jesus did not operate on His own, but let Himself be taught by God (John 8:28). He was in a relationship of

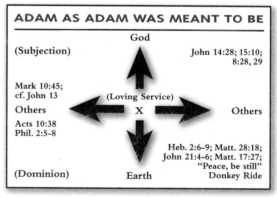

perfect subordination to His Father. He was Adam as God created him to be.

Jesus also had a perfect relationship with His fellow human beings as He walked our world. We observe this relationship with others beautifully illustrated by the foot-washing service in John 13. Jesus "did not come to be served, but to serve" (Mark 10:45). "He went around doing good" (Acts 10:38). He "made himself nothing, taking the very nature of a servant. . . . He humbled himself" (Phil.

2:7, 8). If every person on earth had the spirit and attitude of Jesus, there would be sweet harmony in the loving service each would provide for others. True equality manifests itself in mutual submission and service. Jesus demonstrated in His relationships with others that He was Adam as God had planned for him to be.

It is in His relationship with the environment that the parallels between Jesus and Adam become especially interesting. God created the first Adam to rule over the earth (Gen. 1:26, 28; Heb. 2:6-8). The Second Adam (Jesus) inherited that role from the first by the new creation (verses 8, 9). He fulfilled the original intent God had had for Adam. Thus many of the stories in the Gospels become illustrations of Jesus' dominion over the earth.

The disciples, for example, went fishing on the Sea of Galilee one night, but they caught nothing (John 21:1-3). Why were they fishing at night? Lure fishing takes place in daylight. You want the fish to see the lure, be attracted, and bite into the line. But net fishing works best at night. The fish wanders into the net without even realizing that anything is there. If you have had no luck during the night, the net fisher has one last chance in the early hours of the morning. They can throw the net on the shady side of the boat. A fish enjoying the early-morning sunshine drifts into the shadow of the boat, is blinded momentarily, and *ZZZAAAPPP!* The fish is caught.

But the biblical story has a Man standing on the beach (Jesus—John 21:4, 5). He knew a lot about preaching, but He seemed to know very little about fishing when He called out, "Throw your net on the right side of the boat" (verse 6). Since the disciples weren't stupid, He was clearly inviting them to throw the net on the sunny side of the boat—not a great strategy under ordinary circumstances. But He was no ordinary preacher. This was Adam as God meant for him to be. He had dominion over the fish of the sea (Gen. 1:26, 28)! So 153 fish instantly obeyed Him and swam into the disciples' nets.

A week before His crucifixion Jesus took a ride on an unbroken colt (Mark 11:1-8). If you or I were to try this, the ride would be a short one! But Jesus had dominion "over every living creature that moves on the ground" (Gen. 1:28). He could freely declare, "All authority in heaven and on earth has been given to me" (Matt. 28:18), because He was Adam as Adam was intended to be. Jesus lived perfectly in all three of Adam's relationships: in obedience to God, in loving service to others, and in dominion over the earth and its animals. The image of God was fully restored, not only spiritually, but also socially and physically in Him.

The Adam-Christ typology has some further dimensions. Like the first Adam, the Second Adam had a wayward bride. "I promised you to one husband, to Christ, so that I might present you as a pure virgin to him. But I am afraid that just as Eve was deceived by the serpent's cunning, your minds may somehow be led astray from your sincere and pure devotion to Christ" (2 Cor. 11:2, 3). Paul here compares the church to Eve, carrying the "Second Adam" typology a step further. God put the first Adam to sleep in the garden and made an opening in his side. From that opening came the substance that God used to make the woman (Gen. 2:21, 22). Similarly, the Second Adam was put to sleep (on the cross) and an opening was made in His side (John 19:31-37). From that opening came the substance (water and blood—cf. 1 John 5:6) from which God created the church.

Jesus Christ is all that God had meant Adam to be. Like Adam, He was tempted on the point of appetite (in the wilderness—cf. Matt. 4:1-3). In His temptations He went where the first Adam had failed; but unlike the first, the Second Adam conquered. In overcoming Satan's temptations Jesus passed over the ground of Adam's failure and redeemed it.

On the other hand, Jesus also accepted the consequences of Adam's failure. Because of sin, the first Adam fell under the curse. It afflicted him with nakedness (Gen. 3:10, 11), thorns (verse 18), sweat (verse 19), and death (Gen. 2:17; 5:5). Likewise, on the cross the Second Adam came under the curse of the first Adam. He too was naked (one purpose of crucifixion was humiliation in front of your family and friends—Heb. 12:2), suffered from thorns and the sweat of anguish, and ultimately died.

So we see a great reversal in the experience of Christ. He lived a perfect life in human flesh, though He had to battle the full force of human temptation. Jesus was Adam as Adam was intended to be. On the basis of His perfect life, the human race inherits eternal life and justification. What had been the original Adam's by right of creation Jesus purchased back at infinite cost. At the same time, although He did not deserve it, Jesus carried all the consequences of human sin in His own body on the tree (Rom. 8:3; 1 Peter 2:24). Christ reaped the full force of the curse. As a result, the death and condemnation that the human race inherited from the first Adam is no longer held to its account (Rom. 5:19).

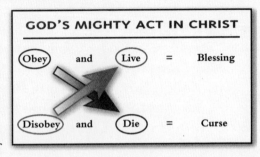

The New Testament understanding of how people get right with God, therefore, is firmly grounded in the fact that Jesus Christ is the new creation, the Second Adam, and the image of God. He is the one who undoes the curse that afflicted the human race as a result of Adam's sin. Christ is the one who overcomes at the same point at which Adam failed. Through experiencing the full history of Adam, Jesus redeems it. As we explore this we begin to get a glimpse of God's greatest and mightiest act. In the process we will discover that these biblical concepts hold the key to authentic, confident Christian faith.

THE REDEEMER OF THE EXODUS

The New Testament presents even stronger connections between the life and experience of Jesus and Israel's experiences during the Exodus, a fact explicitly stated in Luke 9:30, 31: "Two men, Moses and Elijah, appeared in glorious splendor, talking with Jesus. They spoke about his departure, which he was about to bring to fulfillment at Jerusalem." That's a rather odd statement: "They spoke about his *departure,* which he was about to bring to fulfillment at Jerusalem." Since Jesus was in Galilee at this time you would expect Him to talk about His departure to go *to* Jerusalem. But that's not what He said. Instead, He talks about His departure that would be fulfilled "in Jerusalem." The key is in the Greek word behind "departure": *exodos* (which means roughly "the way out").

In Luke 9 Moses and Elijah were talking to Jesus about His "exodus" that He was about to accomplish in Jerusalem. The cross would become a new exodus for the people of God. Just as Israel went down into the water and emerged free from Egypt, so Jesus would die on the cross, go down into the grave, then come out.

It is interesting, then, that the New Testament views the Lord's Supper as parallel to the Jewish Passover (1 Cor. 5:7). When a Jewish family gets together on Passover, it breaks the matzo and recites, "This is the bread of affliction that we experienced in Egypt." But when Jesus breaks the matzo on His last earthly Passover, He says, "This is My body." The cross of Jesus Christ was a new experience of slavery in Egypt. But in addition to this, at the cross Jesus undergoes a new exodus in behalf of His people.

The New Testament also connects baptism to both the Exodus and the cross (Rom. 6 and 1 Cor. 10). Romans 6:3, 4 relates the death, burial, and resurrection of Jesus to baptism. Just as Jesus died, was buried, and rose again, so also in baptism we die to the old nature and rise up to newness of life. When we are baptized, it is as if we die, are buried under the water, and then emerge to live a new life.

New Testament thinking regards the Exodus and baptism as parallel experiences. The Israelites stood on one shore; they then passed through the waters of the Red Sea and came up on the other side. As a result of the Exodus, they were now free. Likewise, through baptism, the cross of Christ becomes a new exodus for the disciple of Jesus (1 Cor. 10:1-11).

The New Moses

In light of what we have seen already it should not surprise us that the New Testament might draw a connection between Moses and Jesus. Jesus not only experienced a new exodus; He was also a new Moses. Let's start with some explicit texts.

Deuteronomy 18:15: "The Lord your God will raise up for you a prophet like me from among your own brothers. You must listen to him." Israel's great leader himself prophesied that a new Moses was coming. Peter clearly understood the prediction to find its fulfillment in Jesus. Acts 3:22-24: "For Moses said, 'The Lord your God will raise up for you a prophet like me from among your own people; you must listen to everything he tells you. Anyone who does not listen to him will be completely cut off from among his people.' Indeed, all the prophets from Samuel on, as many as have spoken, have foretold these days." The passage quotes Deuteronomy 18:15. It not only declares that Jesus fulfills the prediction of a new Moses, but that God inspired the entire history of the Old Testament as a deliberate foreordaining of the life of Jesus Christ.

Having established the Moses-Jesus connection, let's take a look at how the life of Israel's ancient leader parallels that of Jesus. Both Moses and Jesus experienced attempts on their lives as infants (Ex. 1:8-10, 22; 2:1-10; Matt. 2:13-18). Interestingly enough, in both cases it involved a hostile king and not just a random mugger. In each case the ruler saw the child in some way as a threat to the throne. And in each case the king destroyed many babies in an attempt to eradicate that specific one (today we call that "collateral damage"), yet the one who was targeted escaped. The two stories are remarkably parallel and the only stories quite like that in the entire Bible.

Moses is the only person in the Old Testament to see the actual person of God in any way, shape, or form (Ex. 33:20). Israel's deliverer, however, gets to see only God's back—he never sees His face (verses 21-23). John 1:17, 18, however, declares that no one has truly seen God except Jesus. The reason John says that is that Jesus is "in the bosom of the Father" (verse 18, KJV). That means that He has a face-to-face relationship with God. It is in direct contrast to Moses watching God walking away from him. Yet Moses stands out as a type of Jesus, because he is the only figure in the Old Testament who gets to see God at all.

We find many other parallels between Moses and Jesus. Moses fasted for 40 days and then gave the law on a mountain (Ex. 24:18; 34:28). Jesus fasted for 40 days and then went up on a mountain and presented the law of His new kingdom, the Sermon on the Mount (Matt. 4; 5). Moses appointed 70 elders (Num. 11:16-30); Jesus appointed 70 disciples (Luke 10:1). Both Moses and Jesus were glorified on a mountain (Ex. 34:29-35; Matt. 17:1-8). Moses obtained water from the rock (Ex. 17:6; 1 Cor. 10:4), and Jesus speaks about that living water that will flow from Him and from His believers (John 7:37-39). John 3:14 compares Jesus' "lifting up" on the cross with Moses' lifting up of the serpent in the wilderness (Num. 21:8, 9).

The Old Testament collects the writings of Moses into five books, and Matthew—it's easy to see if you have one of those red-letter editions—gathers Jesus' sayings into five sermons. It is not the case in Luke—you will find many of the same sayings scattered all through the book there. But Matthew groups them into five distinct messages. For Matthew, Jesus is clearly a new Moses who reveals the ways of God just as Moses did.

In the Gospel of John Jesus performs seven miracles that parallel the plagues that Moses brought on Egypt. Moses turns water into blood (Ex. 7:17-24)—Jesus transforms water into wine (John 2:1-11). Moses smites the firstborn sons of Egypt (Ex. 11:1–12:32)—Jesus raises Lazarus from the dead (John 11:1-44). Moses brings darkness over the land (Ex. 10:21-29)—Jesus gives sight to a blind man (John 9:1-41). Moses brings sickness on the people (Ex. 9:8-12)—Jesus heals the sick (John 5:2-9), etc. If you work your way through all the miracles in the Gospel of John, you see that they parallel the plagues of Egypt. Jesus is a new Moses, but whereas Moses had a negative effect on Egypt, Jesus has a positive impact on the lives of people. So throughout the New Testament, in a variety of ways, the biblical writers regard Jesus as the one who fulfills the entire experience of Moses as recorded in the Old Testament.

THE NEW ISRAEL

In the New Testament the concept of Jesus as a new exodus and a new Moses is not far from seeing Him as a new Israel as well. We find this comparison most clearly expressed in Matthew. Jesus is Mary's firstborn (in the Exodus story Israel is God's firstborn, Ex. 4:22, 23). Jesus is brought up out of Egypt in order to fulfill the prophecy "out of Egypt I called my son"—an Old Testament reference to the Exodus (Hosea 11:1). Jesus comes out of Egypt in order to fulfill the experience of Israel. He passes through the waters of baptism (Matt. 3; Luke 3), just as Israel went through the waters of the Red Sea (Ex. 14; 15). And just as Jesus spent 40 days in the wilderness (Matt. 4:1-11; Luke 4:1-13), Israel wandered 40 years in the wilderness (Num. 14:33, 34). In the original experience, God gave the law on a mountain (Ex. 19; 20)—Jesus does the same in Matthew 5-7. And He feeds 5,000 in the desert (Matt. 14:13-21), just as Moses provided Israel manna in the desert (Ex. 16). What's Matthew doing here? He's using the language of the past—the mighty acts of God—to set the tone for God's future mighty deeds in Jesus Christ.

So Jesus is the new Israel as well as the new Moses. Living the experience of Old Testament Israel all over again, He is faithful to God, whereas Israel was unfaithful. But Jesus also reaps the consequences of Israel's failure. Remember that in Deuteronomy 28 Moses listed all that Israel would suffer either through obedience or disobedience. Most of the bad things that were to happen to Israel appear in the experience of Jesus as well.

Deuteronomy 28 predicted that a disobedient Israel would be stripped of its wealth and forced to live in poverty (Deut. 28:15-20). Matthew 8:20 tells us that Jesus had nowhere to lay His head. The cursed ones of Deuteronomy 28 were to be "smitten before [their] enemies" (verse 25, KJV), something that certainly took place on the cross. Other curses of Deuteronomy 28 included darkness (Matt. 27:45), being mocked (Mark 15:19, 31), hunger (Matt. 4:2), thirst (John 19:28), and nakedness (Matt. 27:35). With the exception of hunger, all of these met their fulfillment in Jesus' ordeal at the time of the cross.

The climax of the curses in Deuteronomy 28 occurs in verses 65-67. Israel was to be afflicted with an anxious mind and a despairing heart. Jesus experienced the same at a place called Gethsemane (Mark 14:32-42). So we see powerful connections also between the curses of the covenant and the experience of Jesus. He not only relives the life of Israel and redeems it, He also takes up the curses of Israel and experiences them. Thus He is the complete historical counterpart of Israel, redeeming her failures and exhausting the curses that the covenant raised against her.

We will explore the individual and personal significance of all this at the end of the book. But first we must take the time to make the foundation clear. When we have the complete biblical picture in place we will avoid confusion as to how people get right with God. Although building a solid foundation takes time, the quiet confidence that results is well worth the effort.

THE REDEEMER OF THE MONARCHY
THE NEW TEMPLE

The crowning achievement of the monarchy period was the construction of the Temple under Solomon. The Temple, in a real sense, represents the monarchy, just as the tent sanctuary erected at Sinai symbolizes the Exodus and wilderness experiences. When the Jews came back from Babylon they rebuilt the Temple, but Solomon's Temple is the structure that depicts the period of the monarchy.

The New Testament clearly presents Jesus as the successor of the Temple concept. Matthew 12:6: "I tell you that one greater than the temple is here." Jesus claims to be superior to the Temple. Now, according to the rabbis, only one thing was greater than the Temple, and that was the glory of God's presence (called the Shekinah) inside the Temple. So when Jesus said, "One greater than the temple is standing here," He was identifying Himself with the Shekinah glory that indicated God's very presence in the structure.

A further text equating Jesus with the Temple is John 2:19-21. There Jesus says: "Destroy this temple, and I will raise it again in three days." Those who heard Him must have thought, *Man, how can You possibly think You could do such a thing? So far, it's taken us 46 years to build it!* But John clarifies that Jesus referred to the temple of His body. The Shekinah glory dwelt in a human body for about 33 years right here on earth.

In the New Testament, therefore, the sanctuary is wherever Jesus is. Is Jesus located in heaven at the right hand of God? Then there exists a sanctuary or temple in heaven, just as the book of Hebrews indicates. Is there a temple on earth today? According to Paul, yes. He says, "You [plural] are that temple" (1 Cor. 3:17). In 1 Peter 2:5 Peter declares: "You also, like living stones, are being built into a spiritual house to be a holy priesthood." So the church becomes a new temple on earth because Jesus is present in the church. The church becomes a temple because Jesus is in the midst of wherever the church gathers together.

But the temple concept in the New Testament has a third dimension: "Christ in you, the hope of glory" (Col. 1:27). Jesus dwells not only in heaven and in the church, but also in human bodies through the Holy Spirit. In 1 Corinthians 6:19 Paul uses the singular: "Do you not know that your body is a temple of the Holy Spirit, who is in you, whom you have received from God?" All who receive Jesus and are indwelt by the Holy Spirit become body temples. I find this concept to be a marvelous encouragement to godly living.

So in New Testament terms the temple is wherever Jesus is, whether in heaven, in the church, or dwelling in human bodies by the Holy Spirit. Jesus is the full counterpart of the Temple and the priesthood of the monarchy period.

The New King

A common designation of Jesus in the New Testament is "Son of David." In many ways David became *the* representative person for the whole monarchy period. "Son of" in Hebrew can emphasize likeness as well as kinship. Nobody is more like a father than his son will be when he reaches the same age.

The New Testament presents some parallels, then, between the life of Jesus and that of David. For starters, both Jesus and David were beloved sons, and both were born in Bethlehem. In both cases they began their work for God by encountering a giant—Goliath for David, Satan in the wilderness for Jesus. David and Goliath each represented in their person their entire people. In other words, when David killed Goliath, the Israelites beat the Philistines. And when Jesus conquered Satan in the wilderness, He did it in behalf of all of us. His victory over sin becomes ours.

In a most touching episode, David so loved his rebel son Absalom that he was willing to die for him (2 Sam. 18:33). Jesus did exactly that for the whole human race, sons of God through Adam (Luke 3:23-38), when He perished on the cross. Jesus applies the Absalom story to Himself in John 13. When Jesus anticipates betrayal by Judas, He says, "He who shares my bread has lifted up his heel against me" (verse 18). It is a quotation of Psalm 41:9, in which David refers to Ahithophel.

Ahithophel was David's trusted friend and brilliant adviser. When Absalom rebelled against his father, David, Ahithophel decided to join the rebellion, perhaps because he was Bathsheba's grandfather (David had earlier seduced her and had her husband killed). When David learned as he was fleeing Jerusalem that Ahithophel had gone over to Absalom, he said, "God help us! This man is so sharp, he will smell out our every strategy before we can even think it. If we can't find a way to counter his advice to Absalom, we're finished." So he told Hushai, his second best counselor, "You're no use to me here. If you go back to Jerusalem, you can do something to counter the brilliant advice of

Ahithophel. Just urge the opposite of whatever Ahithophel says and see what happens."

So Hushai returned to Jerusalem, and Absalom welcomed him into his court. Ahithophel first gave his advice on the forthcoming battle. Hushai listened to it and then suggested the opposite approach and convinced the rebel king. When Ahithophel saw that Absalom had rejected his advice, he immediately knew that the cause was lost and that he would end up tried as a traitor, so he went home and hanged himself. In John 13 the quotation of Psalm 41 applies the treachery of Ahithophel to the actions of Judas the night that he betrayed Jesus. Judas hanged himself when his arrangement with the religious authorities didn't work out as he had expected. John 13 makes it clear that New Testament writers understood Jesus to be reliving the life and experience of David, Israel's most famous king.

As the "son of David" Jesus also paralleled the life of Solomon, David's royal son. Matthew 12:42 offers an explicit statement: "The Queen of the South will rise at the judgment with this generation and condemn it; for she came from the ends of the earth to listen to Solomon's wisdom, and now one greater than Solomon is here." In this passage Jesus says something similar to what He had said of the Temple earlier in the same chapter: "One greater than the temple is here" (verse 6). Now "one greater than Solomon is here."

The name "Solomon" means "peace"—Jesus is the Prince of Peace. Solomon's career reflected his name. It was a time of peace. David had done all the fighting, and now Solomon presided over all the wealth and prosperity that resulted from his father's victories (see 1 Kings 5:3, 4). So, like Jesus, he was the prince of peace. Solomon was also a king of kings. In addition to his control over the 12 tribes, he also ruled Moab, Ammon, Edom, Philistia, and Syria, among other territories (see 2 Sam. 8:1-14). So Solomon was a king of kings, a designation applied also to Jesus in the New Testament (Rev. 17:14; 19:16).

When Solomon constructed the Temple he had it built without a sound (1 Kings 6:7). In other words, everything was supposed to be fitted together at the construction site, so all hammering and chiseling took place at the quarries and the construction project itself was eerily silent. Jesus built the temple of His church quietly, a kingdom without visible sign. Solomon did not go to the Gentile nations to convert or subdue them. Instead, the glory of his kingdom attracted people of the other nations to come to him, such as the queen of Sheba. When they heard about the wisdom and the wealth of Solomon they visited him to find out more. Likewise, Jesus did not approach the Gentiles. They came to Him—John 12:20, 21 is a good example. Jesus' ministry was one of attraction rather than persuasion.

So the parallels between Jesus and the great kings of Israel portray Him not only as an equivalent to the Temple and the priesthood, but also the true fulfillment of Israel's monarchy. He was both the ideal priest and king. His person united the Mosaic and royal systems.

The New Prophet

We will examine one further tie between Jesus and the monarchy. The New Testament sees Him as the successor to Elijah and the embodiment of Elisha, the two great prophets of the monarchy period. The name Jesus is a cognate of Elisha in Hebrew. The Hebrew name of Jesus means "Yahweh is my Savior," and Elisha means "God is my Savior." So the two names are related. Jesus is a new Elisha.

The parallels are quite detailed. First of all, both Jesus and Elisha began their ministry at the Jordan River. God took up Elijah at the Jordan, and the prophet passed his mantle on to Elisha there (2 Kings 2:9-12), Jesus also received His commission from John the Baptist at the Jordan (Matt. 3:13-17). And who is John the Baptist? "If you're willing to accept it," Jesus says, "he's Elijah" (see Matt. 11:11-15). John came in the spirit and power of Elijah (Luke 1:17), while Jesus manifested the spirit and power of Elisha.

Interestingly enough, Elijah and John the Baptist were both austere figures who dwelled in remote places, sometimes living off the land. They wore rough clothing, and when they encountered people they hollered a lot. Thus they were somewhat frightening, hermit-type individuals. Elisha and Jesus, on the other hand, exhibited more normal lives. They lived in towns (see Matt. 4:13; John 2:12)—Elisha, in fact, resided in the capital city of the northern kingdom of Israel. He had a house that people could stay in, etc. While Jesus was more rural than Elisha, He was not as rustic or extreme as John the Baptist was.

The parallels between Jesus and Elisha go even further. The portrayal of Jesus in the Gospel of John seems deliberately designed to recall the major miracles in Elisha's life. The first of the seven miracles that Jesus did in the Gospel of John involved the transformation of water into wine (John 2:1-11). In 2 Kings 2:19-22 Elisha's first miracle turned polluted water into clean water. The second miracle in each case was restoring a boy to full health: 2 Kings 4:32-37 and John 4:46-54. Then, in John 6, Jesus multiplies barley loaves, something that Elisha did at Gilgal (2 Kings 4:42-44). There seems to be a special connection between the two events, since barley loaves were common to both.

Jesus heals a sick man in John 5:1-15 (the parallel miracles are not in exactly the same order) and Elisha heals Naaman in 2 Kings 5:1-14. Both Elisha and Jesus also do miracles that prevent something from sinking in water: Elisha makes an axhead float (2 Kings 6:4-7), and Jesus walks on the water (John 6:16-21). Then Elisha heals the blindness of the Syrians (2 Kings 6:15-20), and Jesus heals the blindness of the man in John 9. Finally Jesus raises Lazarus from the dead (John 11:1-44). The very last act of Elisha, after his own death, was to restore another man from the dead! It appears that after Elisha was dead and buried, several men opened his grave and tossed a body in (pursued by enemy raiders, they acted in a hurry). When the dead man's body hit the bones of Elisha, the man came to life and got up (2 Kings 13:20, 21).

It seems quite evident, therefore, that people of New Testament times recognized the experience of Elisha as a parallel of that of Jesus. Jesus takes the place that prophets occupied during the monarchy. He is, therefore, the ideal prophet, priest, and king. Thus Jesus assumes the place of Israel not just in the time of the Exodus but also in the monarchy period. As we will see, He relives the whole experience of Israel, including the Exile.

The Redeemer of the Exile

In our previous journey through the Old Testament we started out with the Creation, moved to the Exodus, and then on to the monarchy. Now we turn to the last great period of the Old Testament historical record—Israel's exile to Babylon and return after 70 years.

This time we'll approach the topic a little bit differently. Instead of focusing on parallels scattered throughout the New Testament, we will take a specific New Testament text and see how Paul utilized the Old Testament record of the Exile. In Galatians 3:10-14 he writes: "All who rely on observing the law are under a curse, for it is written: 'Cursed is everyone who does not continue to do everything written in the Book of the Law.' Clearly no one is justified by God by the law, because 'The righteous will live by faith.' The law is not based on faith; on the contrary, 'The man who does these things will live by them.' Christ redeemed us from the curse of the law by becoming a curse for us, for it is written: 'Cursed is everyone who is hung on a tree.' He redeemed us in order that the blessing given to Abraham might come to the Gentiles through Christ Jesus, so that by faith we might receive the promise of the Spirit."

One reason people have difficulty with the apostle's writings is that they often don't read him in the context of the Old Testament. When you look at the whole picture of Paul, including his dynamic and continual allusions to Old Testament ideas and events, his writings become much clearer. In Galatians 3 Paul employs the story of Abraham. Abraham is a character in the Old Testament who became right with God. So Paul suggests, "Let's find out how Abraham got right with God. That will provide a good model for how we also get right with God." Verse 10: "All who rely on observing the law are under a curse, for it is written: 'Cursed is everyone who does not continue to do everything written in the Book of the Law.'" Where is it "written"? In Deuteronomy 27:26. That is the introduction to the blessings and curses of Deuteronomy 28, about which we have already had a lot to say.

So Paul, at this decisive point, moves right into the blessings and curses of the covenant. Now Deuteronomy, as you know, was a covenant with the nation as a whole. And God offers the nation blessing if, as a people, they are faithful to Him. Israel, however, faces a curse if they are unfaithful to God.

Now what happens when the entire nation falls under the curse—when all Israel has failed to obey God? Deuteronomy has an answer. The ultimate curse for the nation is exile (Deut. 28:32-37). The people live among foreigners and no longer have a corporate existence. Normally, exile destroys a nation and is the ultimate curse for a people group.

Now Paul has a problem: Israel, for all practical purposes, is still in exile. Even though many of the people are back in Palestine, Rome actually rules them, not David or one of his descendants. What do you do when the whole nation is in exile? The path of Deuteronomy runs out at a dead end. You come to the end of the Old Testament, and God's people have never been fully reestablished as a nation. The promises of Deuteronomy lack fulfillment. Israel seems to have no future.

To put Paul's question in other terms: "What is the point of Christianity? Why should a Jew consider Jesus? What Jewish significance does being a Christian have?" In Galatians 3:13 he explains it: "Christ redeemed us from the curse of the law by becoming a curse for us, for it is written, 'Cursed is everyone who is hung on a tree.'"

Now a problem we have as Westerners is that we immediately see the situation in individual terms—Christ died for me. And that's not wrong. Paul can say that (Gal. 2:20). But here, he has a much bigger picture in mind. He sees the whole nation, Israel, under a curse. And he asks, "What is God's answer to this big problem? How can He deal with a cursed nation?" The answer he comes up with is that Jesus Christ takes that curse upon Himself. Jesus Himself relives Israel's experience of exile.

In Philippians 2 we come to understand that Jesus exiled Himself from heaven, became a human being, and went even lower than that to slavery and death. Verses 6-8: "Who, being in very nature God, did not consider equality with God something to be grasped, but made himself nothing, taking the very nature of a servant, being made in human likeness. And being found in appearance as a man, he humbled himself and became obedient to death—even death on a cross!" What Paul is saying in Galatians 3 is that in His exile to earth Jesus functions as the representative of Israel, reliving Israel's exile. In Jesus' suffering and death Israel itself comes to an end in His person. So Paul understands the life and death of Jesus as that of a new Israel experiencing a new exile.

Thus Paul's answer to the exile of Israel is the cross of Jesus Christ. That's why we've spent so much time working through the Old Testament. The Old Testament was Paul's Bible. With the Old Testament in mind, every text in the New Testament takes on fresh significance. The Israel of the Old Testament was exiled and, in a sense, the nation was finished. But now, at the cross, an even deeper exile of Israel has taken place. And it's a redeeming exile that would enable Israel to become whole again.

For Paul the stakes here are high. As we have seen in Genesis 12:1-3 God intended that Israel would be a blessing to the nations. But according to Deuteronomy, in order for Israel to be a blessing to the nations it must first become blessed itself. Israel's obedience would not only bring blessing to Israel, but to the whole world. So because Israel failed to achieve the blessing for itself it could not be the conduit through which the blessing of Abraham would reach the world. Here we see the passion behind Paul's theology. For him, to reject Jesus is to give up on Israel. But to find Jesus is to revive hope in the promises made to Abraham.

Galatians 3:13, 14: "Christ redeemed us from the curse of the law by becoming a curse for us. . . . He redeemed us in order that the blessing given to Abraham might come to the Gentiles through Christ Jesus, so that by faith we might receive the promise of the Spirit." If the nation as a whole had failed to bring the blessing to the world, God could redeem those under the curse through the action of the nation's representative: Jesus. In Jesus God accepts Israel as a whole. And in Jesus the promises made to Abraham find their fulfillment, including the promises of blessing to all the nations of the earth.

For the New Testament writers the events that took place at Pentecost (Acts 2) were the sign that the covenant had been fulfilled and that the blessing had come to the Gentiles. At the tower of Babel God had scattered the languages of the world (Gen. 11). When at Pentecost representatives from all over the world miraculously heard the gospel in their own languages (Acts 2:1-11), it became the sign that Genesis 12 was being fulfilled. The blessing of Abraham was now going to the nations.

Whereas God had first intended that the blessing should spread through the obedience of Abraham and Israel, it is now to come through faith in the obedience of Jesus, the new Israel who redeemed the exile of Old Testament Israel. Galatians 3:11: "Clearly no one is justified before God by the law, because, 'The righteous will live by faith.'" Just as Israel had faith in God at the time of the Exodus, so now Paul urges the Galatians to have faith in God in this new exodus in Jesus Christ. The neat thing about faith is that both Jews and Gentiles can get in. You no longer have to be born with the right physical heritage or in the right geographical territory. Instead, you have faith in a mighty act of God.

The deeper perspective of Deuteronomy is that Israel was to be defined all along by its response to God's mighty deeds. As Israel responded to them with obedience and praise they were to be blessed and become the center of blessing to the world. So Paul was not really presenting a different theology than that of the Old Testament—he was going below the surface and showing that faith in Jesus is an act in harmony with the deeper meaning of the Old Testament, what the Old Testament actually meant all along.

For the writers of the New Testament, then, the coming of Jesus was God's greatest and mightiest act. In the person of Jesus Christ the God of the universe walked in human flesh. If this claim is true, it is the most wonderful thing that has ever happened in the history of the human race. It was a mighty act of God, the equal of Creation, the equal of the Flood, the equal of the Exodus—the equal of all that God had done in the experience of Israel.

The personal implications of all that we have covered in this chapter are enormous. They can make all the difference in how we live from day to day. In the concluding chapters of this book (9-11) we will examine on a personal level what it means to have a new history. We will ponder what it means to have a new relationship with God, what it means to live a life of faith. But we must first explore one other dimension of the Old Testament before we can reach that final conclusion.

PART TWO

The Bible and the Rules of Relationship

CHAPTER 6

DESIGNED FOR STABILITY

In the first chapter we noted the fact that the Bible presents itself as the exciting history of a people and their God. It is the story of a God who truly cares as He tries to bring His people into a meaningful relationship with Himself. But a second thing that stands out to anybody who reads the text for the first time is that the Bible has a lot of rules and regulations. It is not very exciting to most people. They would prefer that those rules and regulations were not there. So what is the purpose of the laws of the Bible? Why have rules and regulations if people don't like them?

The Importance of Legal Language
From What God Is Like

One reason the Bible is full of law is that God is a deity of law and order. How do I know that? For starters, the natural world teaches us something about the Person who designed the universe. In practical terms the universe behaves in highly consistent ways. For example, if I hold a pencil in my hand and let go, what happens? The last 10 times I did that it fell to the ground. The pencil never goes up and it never floats in the air. Maybe it's different where you live, but in my experience the law of gravity is still in effect. It tells me that whoever designed our universe is extremely concerned that things will function in a reasonably predictable fashion.

In practical terms, then, the universe is dependable. When you get up in the morning, your shoes are not on the ceiling. I don't know about you, but it would really mess up my mind if I woke up and discovered my shoes up there. I depend on finding them where I left them (which isn't always where my wife wants me to put them). I count on the consistency and reliability of the universe I am living in.

Let me give you another example. How is it possible for me to walk across a room? Every time I take a step I am pushing off the floor, and that requires friction. Now, if you have ever been on an icy lake at just the right temperature, you know that without friction you don't get very far and may even hurt yourself. I depend on friction to get through a day, even when I don't think about it (and I rarely do). When I swing my legs off the bed and onto the floor I am counting on a little friction! Without it, I'm not going anywhere.

Often things get more complex than that. Aviators, for example, play one law against another in order to fly. If you use the law of lift just right you can, in a sense, suspend the law of gravity and move a large airplane full of people through the air. But we count on the law of lift just as much as we count on the law of gravity. If one day air provided no lifting power against a wing, there would be a whole lot of surprises at the airport. But fortunately that too doesn't happen. In practical terms, the laws of the universe are consistent and dependable. And if God designed this universe, then it must be that He is a God of law and order.

From What We Are Like

I believe that God filled the Bible with legal language for a second reason. Human beings themselves are beings of law and order despite the fact that we grumble and complain about rules. We are different than the animals. For example, animals don't lie. If a dog doesn't like you, it doesn't grin. It provides you plenty of warning about its hostility. And if a dog does like you, get ready for some slobber, because there is no way a dog can hold back and hide its feelings of affection.

Dogs don't particularly operate by conscience, either. Have you ever met a dog that felt bad about stealing a piece of meat and decided to return it? We are distinct from animals in our sense of right and wrong. The fact that most human beings have a conscience tells us that God has made us with a definite legal streak. He built in us a need for justice. Have you ever played or watched a pickup game of basketball? Do you know what a do-over is? It's an attempt at fairness. Somebody calls a foul or "traveling" (or "steps"), then an argument starts, and finally everyone decides on a do-over. A do-over says, "Let's act as if this never happened and run the play again."

Why do people argue about calls in basketball? Because of a basic human need for fairness. I remember once as I took down a rebound in basketball and started heading up the court that it looked like a good opportunity for a fast break. Just then an opponent came over and called a foul. My stomach had contacted his elbow. I was incensed. How could my stomach foul his elbow? It made no sense to me at all. And I really got on his case about it. I thought it was a ridiculous call and unfair.

Why do people argue with their spouses? If your spouse is always right, you have no reason to protest. But when you argue, you are questioning the justice of a particular statement or action. So every time we have an argument with our spouses, we confess our belief that justice and fairness are built-in aspects of our beings. We feel the need to live in a universe that is stable, consistent, and based on law.

THE KEY TO STABLE RELATIONSHIPS

If we recognize that law and order are natural to us and to the universe, that still leaves the question Why? Why is it so natural? Why are law and order so important for us? What advantages do we receive for obeying the laws of nature and society? For one thing, law places boundaries around our behavior. Some things are acceptable within a group of people and other things are not. Such boundaries provide security. If you are in a high-crime area, you trust that the locks are strong. At its best, law functions like that. It protects us from ourselves, from our own instability. Without boundaries of some kind, freedom can be a highly destructive thing.

Laws also reveal something about the character of those that make them. Good laws benefit everyone, while bad laws help few if any, or advantage one group at the expense of another. In the words of the American Declaration of Independence, good laws enhance "the pursuit of happiness." Good laws provide a stable environment for growth and development.

COVENANTS AND RELATIONSHIP

Above all else, we need to view law in the context of "relationship." In the absence of relationship "law" tends to become coldhearted and abusive. But within the context of relationship the right kind of law becomes a boundary within which we can experience tremendous freedom. The Old Testament calls the laws of relationship "covenants." The concept of covenant closely resembles the English word "contract." In a "covenant" two parties enter into a relationship of some kind—to build a house, to get married, to go to school. All these things involve a relationship between people or between a person and an institution. The contract defines those relationships and provides security and boundaries for those relationships.

Earlier in this book we talked about the importance of telling and retelling what God has done. Psalm 105:5-10 is one of those rehearsals of what God has done. But an interesting twist makes it a little different than the passages we looked at in the previous section on history.

"Remember the wonders he has done,
    his miracles, and the judgments he pronounced,
O descendants of Abraham his servant,
    O sons of Jacob, his chosen ones.
He is the Lord our God;
    his judgments are in all the earth.
He remembers his covenant forever,
    the word he commanded, for a thousand generations,
the covenant he made with Abraham,
    the oath he swore to Isaac.

He confirmed it to Jacob as a decree,
    to Israel as an everlasting covenant."

Like the recitals of history, this passage begins with a reference to God's marvelous acts. It moves immediately, however, to such concepts as judgment, covenant, and oath. God grounds His mighty deeds in law and covenant. He swore an oath to the pioneers of ancient Israel and said, "Here is how I'm going to treat you as a people."

That's the amazing thing in this passage. God regulates His side of the relationship by covenant just as thoroughly as the human side. In other words, the great God of the universe, the King, the Creator—who by definition could do anything He wanted—chooses to confine Himself by rules and regulations! He does this because He desires to be in relationship with human beings. And He wants us to feel secure in that relationship. So before God ever asked anyone to submit to rules, He first put Himself under those same rules. His action is the ground for our reaction.

That brings us to the rules part. Any covenant stipulates criteria that are binding on both parties. Sometimes young people don't like rules and regulations because they see them as arbitrary, someone else's attempt to control them from the outside. This happens, parents, when you establish rules for your kids that you yourself don't abide by. But the Bible tells us that God's rules flow right out of His own consistent action.

Let's see how this works in a fabulous law passage, Deuteronomy 30:16-19: "For I command you today to love the Lord your God, to walk in his ways, and to keep his commands, decrees and laws; then you will live and increase, and the Lord your God will bless you in the land you are entering to possess. But if your heart turns away and you are not obedient, and if you are drawn away to bow down to other gods and worship them, I declare to you this day that you will certainly be destroyed. You will not live long in the land you are crossing the Jordan to enter and possess. This day I call heaven and earth as witnesses against you that I have set before you life and death, blessings and curses. Now choose life, so that you and your children may live."

Law provides boundaries within which there is freedom. Deuteronomy 30 offers a choice, and it's a life-and-death one. God's desire for Israel was life. He wanted them to "choose life." The rules and regulations do not simply float out there in space—their purpose is to enhance life. Our actions have consequences: obey and live, or disobey and die.

Deuteronomy's message about "blessings" and "curses" is not that far from where we live today. A few years back the bridge in my hometown collapsed. It was a terrible thing for the community because it turned the downtown business section into a dead-end street. And that pretty much destroyed the downtown economically. The merchants no longer had customers. The situation was so desperate that when the local authorities wrote up a contract for a new bridge, the community leaders said, "You must put a date in that contract."

The contract set the date for May 26, about nine months later. And that was a challenge for the builders. So the community leaders put "blessings and curses" in the contract. For every day that the construction company finished the bridge ahead of schedule, the authorities would put $10,000 extra in the builders' pockets. And for every day that completion was late, they would deduct $10,000 from their final payment. You know what? They finished the bridge 26 days early! That is what Deuteronomy means by blessings and curses. A blessing is the reward you get when you fulfill your side of a contract. A curse here is not about swearing—it involves the consequences of not fulfilling the contract. Blessings and curses are motivators.

So law for the Hebrew mind was not cold, formal, or harsh. It was the natural consequence of a living relationship with God. Israel as a people rejoiced in the rules and regulations because they knew that the law also governed God's behavior toward them. You see, the pagan gods weren't like the God of Israel. Pagan deities could wake up on the wrong side of the bed and destroy 10,000 people just because they were in a bad mood. The gods of the other nations lurked behind every tree in the forest. You never knew when you'd get slapped upside the head with them. So to have a God who says,

"I will abide by law," provided incredible security to the Israelites. They knew whom they were dealing with. For them the rules and regulations were a very good thing, and they loved them. Just read Psalm 119: "I delight in your law" (verse 70), "your law is my delight" (verse 77), "Oh, how I love your law!" (verse 97), "your law is my delight" (verse 174).

Israel loved God's laws for still another reason. Every so often some other nation played the bully against them. But with God that was never the end of the story. God's people could take those bullies to the court of His judgment and sue for damages! In fact, the Hebrew term for "lawsuit" appears throughout the Old Testament. Whenever things didn't go the way they were supposed to, God's people could bring a lawsuit.

So the Israelites did not fear law courts or even God's judgment. They did not find law cold and abusive. Instead, they looked forward to divine judgment because they knew that when the judgment day came, God would hear their lawsuit and they were going to win and receive heavy damages from the enemy. Everything would be turned around. The oppressors would go down, and God would vindicate His people.

In the ancient pagan idea of godhood "might makes right." The pagan deities were gods because they were powerful, not because they were always good. The Greek gods, for example, were promiscuous, abusive, and inconsistent. What made them gods then? Raw, unrestrained power. The biggest bully on the street becomes god, so to speak. That's why the Old Testament concept of God, as primitive as it may seem to some today, was such a wonderful advance at that time. The Hebrew Scriptures say that God is mighty because He is right. It turns the pagan concept on its head. God deserves to be God because He is right, not because He is powerful.

The proper rule of law, therefore, is extremely important to a happy society. During recent years, in reaction to the abusive character of law in the Communist era, the rule of law has broken down in Russia. The result is a sense of disorder. No one looks out for society as a whole. Everyone focuses only on their own selfish interests. Moscow, for example, is one of the greenest cities I've ever seen—certainly not what I expected. The problem, though, is that nobody takes care of the greenery, except in the Kremlin itself. In many places the grass grows six feet tall, and because people have worn all kinds of paths through it, the place looks chaotic. One has a sense that nobody cares. You know what happens in that kind of atmosphere? When law and order breaks down in the little things, it creates an atmosphere in which crime and lawlessness flourish.

My hometown is New York City. Crime has always been a major concern there. A few years ago the city elected a new mayor. Without getting into the politics, I just want to note that he brought into office with him an idea that seemed strange at the time. His idea was that "if you allow people to ignore or despise the law in little things, you will lose control in the big things." So instead of focusing primarily on the Mafia and the major criminal elements in the city, he promoted a campaign to make the city an unwelcome place for panhandlers, squeegee people, and grafitti artists. And he faced a storm of criticism right from the start.

What are squeegee persons? They're the ones who come up to your car at a red light and start spraying your windshield, offering to clean a bit of it for a dollar. What happens to those driving the car? They have a feeling of insecurity, a sense of "Hey, wait a minute; don't touch my car!" The action is not wanted, it is forced upon them, and they're even expected to pay for it, with occasional threats if they don't. The result is insecurity and abuse, the sense of being in an unsafe place. Law-abiding citizens feel afraid.

The amazing thing is that by tackling the insecure environment, the whole atmosphere of the city changed. Take away the minor yet obvious abuses of law, and the criminals begin to find things uncomfortable for them. Today you see women walking alone on the streets of Manhattan at 11:00 p.m., something I never saw as a kid. In an atmosphere of respect for law, the major criminals begin to feel insecure and the people retake the streets. No one will claim that all segments of the city have benefited equally from such policies, but all parts of the city seem to be safer and more orderly. It is far better to be ruled by law than by the whims of criminals or dictators.

So the biblical concept of Deity is that He is God because He is right, not because He is powerful. And He is safe because He subjects Himself to the same laws that He expects us to obey. The biblical concept of law is not cold and arbitrary, but is the throbbing heart of a stable society in relationship with a loving God. It is intimately tied to the history of Israel, to its experience with God as a people.

In Deuteronomy 26:1-10 we see this blending of history and law in one of Israel's great confessions of faith. When the Israelites became settled in their land God required them to bring the firstfruits of the harvest in a basket to His holy place and present it to a priest there (verses 1-3). Then they were to recite the mighty acts of God to the priest. "My father was a wandering Aramean, and he went down into Egypt with a few people and lived there and became a great nation, powerful and numerous. But the Egyptians mistreated us and made us suffer, putting us to hard labor. Then we cried out to the Lord, the God of our fathers, and the Lord heard our voice and saw our misery, toil and oppression. So the Lord brought us out of Egypt with a mighty hand and an outstretched arm, with great terror and with miraculous signs and wonders" (verses 5-8). In the Old Testament the laws have to do with responding to God's actions in behalf of His people. The keeping of the law and the rehearsing of His mighty deeds were two sides of the same coin.

The problem with covenant and law is that every one of us has a deep sense inside that we have not lived up to our own inner rules, much less those set by God. We have failed to live up to our own built-in need for justice. When I declare, "You shouldn't have done that," what am I saying? That what you are doing is not right for you. I am passing judgment on your actions. But if I think it's not right for you, then it's not right for me either. Deep down inside I hold myself accountable to the same rules I point out to others. And that leaves me in a discouraging situation.

Romans 2:1-3: "You, therefore, have no excuse, you who pass judgment on someone else, for at whatever point you judge the other, you are condemning yourself, because you who pass judgment do the same things. Now we know that God's judgment against those who do such things is based on truth. So when you, a mere man, pass judgment on them yet do the same things, do you think you will escape God's judgment?" Sobering thought. Paul here picks up on the idea that when we criticize other people we are really condemning ourselves. The more we castigate others, the more we find ourselves weighed down with our own sense of failure.

The Bible teaches, therefore (and experience seems to confirm), that the greatest of all human needs is to be counted right in the end. We long, when our whole life experience is summed up, for some great judge in the sky to put a hand on our shoulder and say, "You did OK, buddy. Everything is going to be all right." What hope do we have that we might actually experience such affirmation? The answer lies in a deeper look at the Bible's concept of covenant, which we will do in the next two chapters.

CHAPTER 7

THE OLD TESTAMENT CONCEPT OF LAW

It was a hopeless case, but the lawyer didn't give up. He paced back and forth, seemingly oblivious to the muffled sounds of laughter in the gallery. I was in the gallery that day in support of a church member who had been in the wrong place at the wrong time. As we waited in the gallery for his case to come up we got to observe this drunk-driving case play itself out in the courtroom.

The police officer carefully laid out the evidence against the defendant. The officer had been called to the scene of the accident on a day when light snow had covered the ground. The accident had occurred by the bridge at the edge of a small town. When the investigating officer arrived, he found a car smashed into the bridge abutment. The impact had compressed the front of the car about 18 inches (about a half meter), suggesting a crash speed of at least 30 miles (50 kilometers) per hour, and pinned the driver behind the wheel of the car. The defendant was "drunk as a skunk." The officer also observed tire tracks in the snow indicating that the car had been traveling along the sidewalk for at least 120 feet (35 meters) before striking the abutment of the bridge.

The police officer concluded from the evidence that the defendant had been driving the vehicle at the time of the accident and that the accident had occurred because of the driver's inebriated condition. He recommended a large fine and a six-month suspension of the defendant's driver's license on the ground of DUI, driving under the influence of alcohol. With some amusement I wondered what kind of case the defense attorney would try to make. It certainly looked like a hopeless case to me.

But the defense lawyer was undaunted. Immediately rising, he began pacing back and forth before the judge, waving his arms and speaking in an animated voice. He argued that the defendant was not drunk at the time of the accident. Instead, while driving through town, he had swerved to avoid an oncoming vehicle, hitting the bridge abutment instead. In pain and depressed on account of the accident, he had reached for the bottle of alcohol that he had been bringing home and drank some to soothe the pain!

The judge labored with some difficulty to keep a straight face. He pointed out that the tire tracks in the snow did not indicate any swerving—that the vehicle had proceeded straight down the sidewalk for 120 feet, much more consistent with a drunken driver than with a sober one trying to avoid an accident. Although the judge commended the lawyer for his creativity, he said that he didn't buy his story for even one second.

Hardly deflated from his first attempt, the defense lawyer tried a totally new tack. First he argued that the state had no proof that his client was in fact the driver of the car in question. Then he suggested that the actual driver of the car had left the scene of the accident after it occurred. The defendant then wandered by "drunk as a skunk" and climbed into the driver's seat of the car for shelter from the cold. His stomach swelled up a bit from the alcohol, and he became pinned behind the wheel.

By now the gallery was beginning to get out of control with suppressed giggling. But the judge didn't call for order, as he was having a hard time controlling his own mirth. Finally he interrupted the lawyer's pacing and gesturing.

"Mr. ———, I *do* not believe your story—any of your stories. But I have to confess, in my 20 years on this bench I have heard many things and did not expect any surprises today. But you have taken your craft to new levels of creativity. Nevertheless, I find your two defenses completely incredible. The defendant is fined a total of

$250 [25 years ago that was *real* money], and his license is suspended for six months."

"I appeal this decision, Your Honor," the defense lawyer brazenly blurted out.

"Then you are to appear before the appeals court within 14 days to show cause why an appeal should be heard," the judge replied. With that comment he rapped the gavel on his desk and turned his head quickly, covering his mouth so the audience couldn't see his smile.

It's no fun to take a hopeless case to court. No matter what you say or how well you argue it, you end up facing bitter penalties. That is why many people fear the judgment seat of God. They are afraid that the evidence is overwhelming against them and that the only possible outcome will be a negative one. But that is not how the Hebrews thought about judgment day. For them it was something to look forward to. Let's take a closer look at how the Old Testament deals with matters of law and judgment.

The fundamental purpose of law and covenant in the Bible, as we have seen, is to regulate and govern relationships. It's not cold and heartless. Law is all about the joy of life with other people. And it is about the joy of being in relationship with God. God's relationship with His people is grounded in legal safeguards.

The Old Testament expresses the legal side of God's relationship to His people in three basic ways. The English equivalents are the words "covenant," "righteousness," and "judgment." We could look at additional legal terms in the Old Testament, but for the purposes of a short book these three will help us sum up the big picture.

1. Covenant in the Old Testament

We have already discussed this term in general, but now we need to see how the text of the Old Testament itself uses it. The legal language of the rest of the Old Testament (and even of the New) is grounded on the concepts introduced in the book of Deuteronomy. Deuteronomy 4:7, 8: "What other nation is so great as to have their gods near them the way the Lord our God is near us whenever we pray to him? And what other nation is so great as to have such righteous decrees and laws as this body of laws I am setting before you today?"

As we observed earlier, the pagan world was (and is) an extremely insecure one. The gods lurked behind every tree, waiting to torment you. If you have ever gone on the Norwegian boat ride at Walt Disney World you have experienced a glimpse of what I am talking about. That ride features the terrors of the pagan world of ancient Norway, with its weird, misshapen creatures lurking in the forest. In our postmodern world we often romanticize the pagan gods, but in reality paganism produced a fearful and apprehensive existence. And that world still exists in the minds of some people in places such as New Guinea and rural Africa. It is a very frightening way to live.

This background helps us understand the boasting in Deuteronomy 4. What other nation has a God like this? What other people has a deity as consistent and dependable as the God of Israel? The law-and-order side of Yahweh was one of the best things about Him. You could depend on Him. Yahweh was willing to be bound by the same rules and regulations that He asked Israel to follow. And that provided security for them.

God's laws are an intimate part of His covenant. Deuteronomy 4:13: "He declared to you his covenant, the Ten Commandments, which he commanded you to follow and then wrote them on two stone tablets." The basis for the legal language of the Old Testament, including the Ten Commandments, is the covenant. Scripture expresses the covenant in terms of what God is willing to do and what He wants His people to do. It both lays out the good life and describes how God reacts to various situations and how His people are to respond to Him. The covenant is not arbitrary or abusive.

The nice thing about it is that Israel's relationship with God did not depend on the nation's performance. Whenever relationships rely on the other party's behavior, the relationship is inherently unstable. Notice what Deuteronomy 7:7-9 says: "The Lord did not set his affection on you and choose you because you were more numerous than other peoples, for you were the fewest of all peoples. But it was because the Lord loved you and kept the oath he swore to your forefathers that he brought you out with a mighty hand and redeemed you from the land of slavery, from the power of Pharaoh king of Egypt. Know therefore that the Lord your God is God; he is the faithful God, keeping his covenant of love to a thousand generations of those who love him and keep his commands."

Wow! God did not commit Himself to Israel because they were powerful and numerous, or because they were better than others. No, He pledged Himself to them because He was keeping His covenant. Did Israel deserve it? Not particularly. In fact, they were pretty messed up. Look at their behavior after God rescued them from Egypt. After every good thing imaginable happened to them, they were still a major pain to deal with. The basis for God's kindness to them was not their performance, but His promises to Abraham.

Israel's security in its relationship with God had its basis in the fact that God told them ahead of time how He was going to behave, and then He did exactly that. He submitted Himself to the same laws that He laid out for them. It is as if God were saying, "I will be exactly what I said I would be. When I give you My laws, I will follow them first. I am not asking you to do anything that I am not willing to do." We may be uncomfortable with some of the penalties laid out for disobedience in the Old Testament, but God held Himself accountable to the same rules of behavior. And it provided tremendous security in a tremendously frightening and precarious world. The good news is that an understanding of the legal side of the Bible can provide similar security in the post-September 11 world of today.

Deuteronomy 30:15, 16: "See, I set before you today life and prosperity, death and destruction. For I command you today to love the Lord your God, to walk in his ways, and to keep his commands, decrees and laws; then you will live and increase, and the Lord your God will bless you in the land you are entering to possess." Is God being arbitrary here, laying out rules that we had better obey or else?

No. He is saying, "Walk in My ways." God has already obeyed. He is doing what He is asking us to do. The Lord is not an Adolf Hitler in jeans. The covenant is ultimately an expression of who God is. His call to obedience is a summons to be like Him. And this covenant was at the root of Israel's relationship with God.

2. Righteousness in the Old Testament

The next key word we need to look at is "righteousness." What is righteousness? Well, first of all, it is simply whatever God does. Psalm 71:16-24: "I will come and proclaim your mighty acts, O Sovereign Lord; I will proclaim your righteousness, yours alone. . . . My tongue will tell of your righteous acts all day long, for those who wanted to harm me have been put to shame and confusion." According to the psalmist, the mighty acts of God define what righteousness is—that is, righteousness is whatever God does. But how do we know that God's actions are what we would consider righteous? Because they are in harmony with the covenant. God's actions are righteous because He does exactly what He said He would do. He keeps His commitments.

Deuteronomy 24:10-13: "When you make a loan of any kind to your neighbor, do not go into his house to get what he is offering as a pledge. Stay outside and let the man to whom you are making the loan bring the pledge out to you. If the man is poor, do not go to sleep with his pledge in your possession. Return his cloak to him by sunset so that he may sleep in it. Then he will thank you, and it will be regarded as a righteous act in the sight of the Lord your God." What is a righteous act? It is behavior in harmony with the covenant. If you do what the covenant says, you are a righteous person. You are doing the right thing. For the Old Testament, righteousness is action in conformity with the covenant. It is modeling one's life on God's righteousness, on His character.

Isaiah 56:1: "This is what the Lord says: 'Maintain justice and do what is right, for my salvation is close at hand and my righteousness will soon be revealed.'" Here God tells us to do what is right. Why?

Because He is about to do what is right, and you want to be on His side when He does that. So we can express the Old Testament concept in two ways. One consists of behavior in harmony with the covenant, and the other models itself on God's actions. But in practice the two definitions of righteousness are the same because God is always faithful to His covenant. When we do what the covenant asks we are righteous, and when we do what God does we are also righteous. Both of those are true.

3. Judgment in the Old Testament

Anyone who has ever faced charges in a courtroom knows the fear that the word "judgment" can instill in us. But if earthly courts create fear, how much worse would it be to stand before God's judgment seat? Nevertheless, the Old Testament is clear that He is a God of judgment. And His judgment is based on righteousness. The purpose of God's judgment is to determine whether or not righteousness has taken place. Has the behavior under scrutiny been in harmony with the covenant or not?

We catch the flavor of this kind of judgment in the history books of the Old Testament. They covered the sweep of history and assessed the behavior of both king and people. The biblical writers defined the good kings by their observance of the laws of Deuteronomy and encouraged the people to do the same. The evil kings ignored the laws of Deuteronomy and sometimes even led the people to worship other gods. In the prophetic books kings also came under judgment (see Jeremiah, for example), but the prophets tended to critique Israelite society as a whole. They assessed the behavior of the whole people in the light of the covenant. Did Israel behave in harmony with the covenant or not? And what was the prophets' usual answer? Not!

The Bible depicts two types of judgment: investigative and executive. Investigative judgment asks the question Has righteousness been done or not? Investigative judgment researches the situation, seeks to find the facts. It gathers evidence regarding what actually took place and then compares that behavior with the standards set in the covenant. And you can't really make a full and final determination until all the facts are in. That's why the process of investigation is important.

Executive judgment, on the other hand, sets things right. It is about ensuring fairness. In the ancient situation the king was to get the facts and then rectify the situation. So executive judgment is both positive and negative. It rewards righteousness and punishes unrighteousness. The Old Testament often describes executive judgment in terms of blessings and the curses. If righteousness had been done, it received blessings as a reward. But if righteousness had not occurred, curses were the result. Righteousness consists of actions in harmony with the covenant. Judgment decides whether or not such actions harmonize with the covenant and then applies the appropriate consequences.

Let's see these ideas at work in some actual texts. First, we'll start with a judgment psalm, Psalm 72. I pointed out earlier that the king of Israel represented Yahweh to the people and the people to Yahweh. So the king's behavior often became the key to how God would treat the nation. Notice the king's role in verses 1-4: "Endow the king with your justice, O God, the royal son with your righteousness. He will judge your people in righteousness, your afflicted ones with justice. The mountains will bring prosperity to the people, the hills the fruit of righteousness. He will defend the afflicted among the people and save the children of the needy; he will crush the oppressor."

When the psalmist requests God to "endow the king with your justice" and "righteousness," he is actually saying, "Endow the king with faithfulness to the covenant." The king is to act the way God does. The next verse makes it clear that the king is the judge of the people. Back then they didn't have a separate judicial and executive branch of government. To employ United States terminology, the king was not only the president but also the chief justice of the Supreme Court. The king's role in Israel was to judge according to the covenant—to judge righteously. He must defend the afflicted, nourish the needy, and crush the oppressor.

Isaiah 3:13-15 sounds a similar theme, but this time God assumes the role of the king in setting the wrongs right. "The Lord takes his place in court; he rises to judge the people. The Lord enters into judgment against the elders and leaders of his people: 'It is you who have ruined my vineyard; the plunder from the poor is in your houses. What do you mean by crushing my people and grinding the faces of the poor?' declares the Lord, the Lord Almighty." Here the rulers and the bureaucrats are abusing the people, so God steps in to do what the king should have done, and that is to bring justice to the exploited. As a result, Israelites came to rejoice in God's judgment, because it would set the inequities of life right, deliver the poor and the oppressed, and make sure the oppressors received their own reward.

What is the role of a righteous government according to this text? Scripture considers a government righteous when it protects the weak and the oppressed. A righteous government stops actions that are out of harmony with the covenant. We learned in the run-up to World War II that diplomacy without teeth behind it is inadequate to deal with an oppressor such as Hitler. A wimp cannot run God's ideal government. Such a government actively enforces the covenant so that the poor and the weak can live in peace and achieve the kind of life that God has in mind for everyone. And that was what the king was supposed to do in ancient Israel.

Let me summarize this quick review of the legal language of the Old Testament. First of all, in the Old Testament covenant regulates relationships. It is the basis on which people interact with each other and with God. As such, the covenant provides security for those relationships. Second, righteousness is not an abstract concept. It's very practical and concrete. Righteousness consists of deeds that reflect the principles of the covenant. Last, judgment assesses whether the covenant is being obeyed or not, and rewards accordingly.

Someone might say that none of this sounds very loving at first glance. But that is a misunderstanding of the Hebrew approach to life. The Hebrew worldview that we see in the Bible is valuable because it is very practical. Hebrews were never content simply to say, "Love everybody." Instead they said, "Do this, and this, and this, and you will be loving." We need to understand the practical Hebraic concept of righteousness before we can grasp the incredible joy of the gospel expressed in the New Testament.

CHAPTER 8

THE NEW TESTAMENT CONCEPT OF LAW

As I was putting the finishing touches on this book, I made a short trip to the Netherlands for a major conference of church employees. After I arrived in Amsterdam and reached the conference site some two hours away, I sat down to eat supper. Another speaker I had met before came over and said, "What do you think of the news that is happening in America?"

"What news?" I said.

"You know," he said, "the four passenger planes that crashed."

"Four planes crashed?" I couldn't believe my ears. When had four passenger planes ever gone down on the same day and in the same country?

"Yes," he said, "two of them hit the World Trade Center in New York and another crashed into the Pentagon in Washington. The World Trade Center collapsed."

I didn't know whether to believe him or not. It sounded like science fiction or some movie plot. "This doesn't make any sense to me," I told him.

"It's true," he insisted. "Go upstairs when you're done. They have CNN on a big screen."

Hurriedly I finished supper and dashed upstairs to find a room with more than 200 chairs and a giant screen with live feed from CNN in the United States. I couldn't believe my eyes. It depicted a view of the World Trade Center from midtown Manhattan, with the tower to the right smoking from the top floors. As I watched, an airplane appeared out of the right side of the screen and slammed into the tower on the left, with a ball of fire spewing out the opposite side. Shortly after that I saw the video of the two towers crashing down upon themselves, carrying any and all occupants to a certain death.

I couldn't get those images out of my mind. After all, I had been born and raised in New York City. The twin towers were so much a part of the city that my mind and my heart kept telling me this was only TV, a movie about something that wasn't really happening. But a few days later, on my return to the United States, we passed New York City at about 30,000 feet, and the smoke still rose from the southern tip of Manhattan Island. It had happened.

In addition to a massive rescue mission, the authorities immediately put hundreds, probably thousands, of investigators to work. They were seeking answers to a number of questions. Who masterminded the attacks? How did the hijackers get past airport security and seize control of the planes? How was United States intelligence caught so completely off guard? What could the nation do to prevent similar attacks in the future? (I discussed some of these issues in *The Day That Changed the World* [Hagerstown, Md.: Review and Herald Pub. Assn., 2002].)

Investigators sifted through the rubble at both sites, looking for clues of who might have done such terrible things. They searched for the two kinds of black boxes that would provide information about the final moments of the doomed airplanes. The voice recorders could indicate if there had been some struggle for control of the cockpit. Data recorders would indicate changes in altitude and speed, and how and when someone aboard the aircraft used various pedals and steering mechanisms. Investigators also went over passenger manifests to find out who might have hijacked each of the planes and how they might have gotten weapons onto them. They interviewed ground personnel who had checked in the passengers, performed the security checks, and handled the baggage. Other investigators monitored recordings of every phone call that went to and from the hijacked planes.

After tracing the likely suspects, more investigators ransacked the apartments and the hotel rooms where the suspects had stayed the night before, looking for clues. They examined the rental cars that had brought the hijackers to the various airports. Law agents interviewed friends, relatives, and neighbors, trying to learn who might have supported the hijackers in their preparations, and who might be capable of committing a similar act in the future. Systematically they checked the phone and travel records of each hijacker.

The goals of the massive investigation were to find out who had committed these dastardly deeds, how they had done them, and who had supported them in carrying out the operations. In a society grounded in law, careful investigation always precedes punishment. It is considered just as evil to imprison the innocent as to let the guilty go free. Eventually the authorities determined that the al-Qaeda organization of Osama bin Laden, supported by the Taliban government of Afghanistan, had been responsible for the attacks.

The conspirators and their supporters who remained alive after the attacks then became the object of an international campaign to "execute" justice. American and other forces secured bases and supplies in many nations, then brought commandos and crack military and police units into the region. Ships, aircraft, helicopters, and ground vehicles moved against the Taliban and the terrorists. Governments froze the assets of all known terrorists. "Dead or alive!" and "Never again!" became headlines in newspapers around the world.

The Old Testament concepts of investigative and executive judgment, therefore, are alive and well in today's world. As in other areas, God condescends to behave in ways that are predictable and dependable within the human context. In these areas the language of the New Testament is consistent with the Old. The definitions of legal words in the Old Testament tend to be the same in the New as well. Our understanding of the Old Testament provides the foundation for comprehending the New. We will go on to see how these matters of covenant, righteousness, and judgment affect our lives even today.

Some readers may have come this far and still wonder what difference all this is going to make. And the question is fair. We have learned to expect quick answers to life's problems. And in a technological age we can quickly resolve many of life's difficulties by applying some new technology. But in the matters of mind and spirit, instant answers often do more harm than good. They can lead us down unproductive sidetracks.

The goal of this book is not spiritual aspirin that enables us to feel good for a few hours but doesn't make a difference in our lives long-term. Instead, I seek to provide an unshakable foundation for secure living that can stand the test of time—the only way to permanent change. Such a foundation must be deep, solid, rightly put together. It requires the accumulation of a certain body of knowledge. We are almost there as we head to a conclusion that has the power to change the world. In the process we are about to discover why so many people have found the faith of the Bible worth dying for.

1. Covenant in the New Testament

The New Testament takes up the Old Testament language of covenant. Let's take a look at a few texts beginning with Matthew 26:28. Just before His crucifixion, Jesus eats one last meal with His disciples, the Last Supper. He takes a cup of grape juice and pronounces over it, "This is my blood of the covenant, which is poured out for many for the forgiveness of sins." The blood of "the" covenant.

"The" is a very small and common word, but sometimes it carries huge implications. In this case, it implies that the person reading or hearing it already has a context. If Jesus had said, "This is the blood of 'a' covenant," the disciples might have replied, "OK, what kind of covenant are You going to tell us about?" But when Christ talks about "the" covenant, He indicates that it is a covenant that they are already familiar with, one that they already understand.

In this case Jesus had even more in mind. He was saying that the cup represented the blood of the one and only covenant, that it was the blood of *the* covenant. Now what covenant could this possibly be? The supper Jesus was eating with His disciples was not just any gathering—it was a Passover meal. It celebrated the fundamental event of the Old Testament, the Exodus.

So Jesus participates in the Passover with His disciples, reviewing the events of the Exodus, then declares, "This is the blood of *the* covenant." What blood is He talking about? The blood of the lamb over the doorposts in the Exodus. And what did that blood do? It saved God's people from death and slavery. The blood symbolized the difference between their whole existence before and everything that came after—the decisive turning point. So at the Last Supper Jesus was announcing a new mighty act of God, a new exodus.

And *the* covenant of the Exodus was the covenant with Abraham, the one going all the way back to Eden. So Jesus' death on the cross would not create a covenant different than the one that already existed. The New Testament uses the language of new covenant, but it is not a different covenant. The new covenant is based on the same covenant as the Old Testament. There is no fundamental break between the two. The New Testament picture of Jesus builds directly on the Old Testament concept of covenant.

Romans 10:8: "But what does it say? 'The word is near you; it is in your mouth and in your heart,' that is, the word of faith we are proclaiming." What does Paul quote here? It is a passage from Deuteronomy, but not just any part of the book—it is Deuteronomy 30, the part about the blessings and the curses. Paul here quotes from *the* covenant, not from some new and different covenant. And he claims that the gospel he is preaching is one and the same with the covenant God gave to Moses in Old Testament times.

Now in the book of Romans Paul is arguing with Jewish opponents who reject the gospel as Paul understands it. People often think that the apostle's gospel created a gulf between himself and Judaism. In fact, just four verses before this Paul said that Christ is the end of the law. But whatever he meant by "end" in verse 4 (the two main possibilities are "goal" and "termination") he is not abolishing the old covenant. Nor is he offering a different covenant. When Christ becomes the end of the law, He is obeying the covenant in doing so. Paul claims that his own preaching is in harmony with the Old Testament covenant.

So what, according to Paul, was God doing when He sent Jesus? He was being faithful to the covenant as He had been all along—*the* covenant, not some new one. Luke 1:67-72: "His father Zechariah was filled with the Holy Spirit and prophesied: 'Praise be to the Lord, the God of Israel, because he has come and redeemed his people. He has raised up a horn of salvation for us in the house of his servant David (as he said through his holy prophets of long ago), salvation from our enemies and from the hand of all who hate us—to show mercy to our fathers and to remember his holy covenant.'"

An angel has just informed Zechariah that his child and that of another are the basis of a new and mighty act of God. And just as in the previous mighty deeds, God is once again remembering His covenant. In Hebrew thinking, remembering has more to do with acting on what you already know than simply recalling something you've forgotten. When God remembers His covenant, it is as if He said to Himself, "I am going to obey this covenant as I've never obeyed it before." And what does He do? He sends Jesus. To be born in Bethlehem. To live a perfect life for 33 years. To die on the cross and be raised from the dead. In sending Jesus God is remembering His holy covenant.

And which covenant? Zechariah continues in Luke 1:73-75: "The oath he swore to our father Abraham: to rescue us from the hand of our enemies, and to enable us to serve him without fear in holiness and righteousness before him all our days." The priest is saying that in the birth of these two babies God is remembering the covenant. He is going all the way back to Genesis 12 and declaring, "Now I am going to do it! Now comes the seed of Abraham! Now comes the salvation that I promised all along."

You see, it was the conviction of the New Testament writers that God had finally come to answer the big question mark we call the Old Testament, that collection of books that constantly looked forward to God's mighty acts that for some reason had never come to completion. Now, *the* mighty, ultimate act of God is finally here. In the Christ event we have the fulfillment of everything that God promised in the Old Testament. Whatever the gospel is, it is based on the same covenant as the Old Testament. The Christ event is God's action in harmony with that covenant. Lots of stuff happened in the Old Testament that wasn't ideal, but God was working in it, preparing the world for what He was going to do in Christ.

2. Righteousness in the New Testament

Now, if the Christ event is God's action in harmony with the covenant, what would the Old Testament call it? Righteousness. The gospel is the revelation of God's righteousness—in other words, God's actions in harmony with the covenant. And this is front-row center in the New Testament's outline of God's mighty deed in Christ. Look at Romans 1:16, 17: "I am not ashamed of the gospel, because it is the power of God for the salvation of everyone who believes: first for the Jew, then for the Gentile. For in the gospel a righteousness from God is revealed, a righteousness that is by faith from first to last, just as it is written: 'The righteous will live by faith.'"

The gospel is nothing less than a revelation of God's righteousness. The gospel proclaims a mighty act of God in harmony with the covenant. It's a revelation of how faithful He was to the covenant. What God did in Jesus Christ was not arbitrary, but was part of a long-term, committed relationship with the human race. It was designed to bring the stability of God into the inconsistency of human experience.

Paul continues on the theme of God's righteousness in Romans 3:21-26. Verse 21: "But now a righteousness from God, apart from law, has been made known, to which the Law and the Prophets testify." In this text we see why people struggle with the meaning of the gospel. Righteousness, by definition, means action in harmony with the covenant. Yet in Romans 3:21 this righteousness comes from God "apart from law" yet testified to by "the Law." Apparently there exists a faithfulness to the covenant that is apart from law, yet it is in harmony with "the" law.

The law in Romans 3:21 (with the definite article) is actually a reference to the five books of Moses. Ancient Jews often referred to what we call the Old Testament as "The Law and the Prophets." "The Prophets" summed up the rest of the Old Testament outside the Pentateuch, the five books of Moses. So Paul is saying that this "apart from law" righteousness does not contradict the Old Testament. In Christ God finds a way to rescue those who have failed to keep the law as a principle of life. But in doing so He is acting in harmony with the Old Testament.

Now if God makes this righteousness from Himself known apart from law, how does He do so? Verses 20-22: "No one will be declared righteous by observing the law. . . . Instead, God's righteousness comes through the faith of Jesus Christ to all who believe" (author's translation). The essential "contradiction" of the gospel then, at least to the Western mind-set, is this: the gospel is a revelation of God's righteousness, which by definition is faithfulness to the covenant, but that revelation comes to us apart from law. Thus God finds another way to save us than the "obey and live" principle of Deuteronomy. But this other way does not contradict the Old Testament since, as we have seen, we can find it there as well. This "apart from law" is not apart from the Old Testament. Whatever it is, it's something the Old Testament agrees with too.

Paul has already said (Rom. 3:20) that we do not achieve righteousness (being counted right before God in the judgment) by observing the law, since no one has ever been able to achieve such perfect righteousness. He then repeats this point in verse 23: "For all have sinned in the past and continually fall short of the glory of God" (author's translation). Not only is our past record messed up before God, but even our best efforts in the present fall short of His standards (not to mention our own, when we are being really honest with ourselves).

But Paul declares that God manifests His righteousness in the middle of our mess *"through the faith of Jesus Christ"* (verse 22, author's translation). What does the "faith of Jesus Christ" mean? He elaborates on this remedy in verse 24: *"And [all] are justified* [same Greek word as "righteousness"] *freely by his grace through the redemption that came by Christ Jesus."* God's mighty act of righteousness comes to us completely free of charge because of the debt (to God's law) Christ Jesus has fully paid. God sent His Son Jesus to this earth to exercise the faithfulness to His law that Israel (and we too) had failed to exhibit.

Verses 25, 26: "God presented him [Jesus] as a sacrifice for atonement, through faith in his blood. He did this to demonstrate his justice [righteousness], because in his forbearance he had left the sins committed beforehand unpunished—he did it to demonstrate his justice [righteousness] at the present time, so as to be just and the one who justifies those who have faith in Jesus." The cross, above all else, reveals God's righteousness, His faithfulness to the original covenant with Abraham. God was never acting so "righteously" as when He sent Jesus to the cross. He found a way at the cross to justify the ungodly and still be faithful to His covenant.

So in the New Testament we see God behaving completely in harmony with the covenant when He dispatches Jesus to live and die in our place. It is in harmony with the Old Testament covenant, yet it comes to us apart from the principle of "obey and live" that is at the root of the realities of this universe. As C. S. Lewis put it in *The Complete Chronicles of Narnia,* God overcame the consequences of reality with the "deeper magic" of Christ's self-sacrifice. The Lord found a way to justify the ungodly and still be faithful to His covenant.

3. JUDGMENT AND THE NEW TESTAMENT

The New Testament doesn't stop with words such as covenant and righteousness. The whole Old Testament concept of final judgment also appears in what happened at the cross. John 12:31, 32: "Now is the time for judgment on this world; now the prince of this world will be driven out. But I, when I am lifted up from the earth, will draw all men to myself." This passage states that in some sense God's judgment on the world took place when Jesus hung on the cross.

Now everything we have covered in this book so far starts to come together. The cross becomes the climax of all God's mighty acts throughout history. At the cross Jesus becomes the new Israel, the Second Adam, and the Son of David. Jesus Christ in His life relived the history of the Old Testament, Israel's history. Then at the cross He reaped the consequences of Israel's failure. On the cross God's judgment against Israel, for centuries of unfaithfulness to the covenant, was exercised in the person of Jesus. Taking its place, Jesus hung on the cross as Israel's representative.

Through the centuries people have tried to understand the full significance of the cross. But this much we know. At the cross God somehow put Jesus in the place where Israel was and exercised His judgment against the nation. And it is not just any judgment—it was *the* judgment of the whole world. It is God's final word on everything that matters.

You could say that the final judgment went into session one Friday afternoon in Jerusalem. Old Testament Israel—in fact, the entire human race (going back to Adam)—was summed up in the person of Jesus Christ. In His person He was Adam, Moses, Israel, David—everybody. And in His person, God condemned Israel. As God looked down on the human race in the person of Jesus, He saw in Him millenniums of unfaithfulness to the covenant. God then poured out on its representative, Jesus, the curse—the condemnation—that not only Israel but the whole human race deserved.

Romans 8:3: "For what the law was powerless to do in that it was weakened by the sinful nature, God did by sending his own Son in the likeness of sinful man to be a sin offering. And so he condemned sin in sinful man." "What the law was powerless to do in that it was weakened by the sinful nature" is a poignant statement of why Deuteronomy failed. Life could not come from human obedience because human beings were "weakened by the sinful nature."

The law had no power to save because the whole human race had failed to obey it. Now all the sin of the human race was placed upon the Son of God and condemned in the death of Christ.

But, thankfully, God didn't complete the judgment on Friday. His judgments are always twofold. They are both positive and negative. So the judgment at the cross adjourned and rested over the Sabbath. It then reconvened on Sunday morning, and God took a second look at the human race. And in His second look, what did He see? He saw Adam as Adam was intended to be (in Christ). He saw Moses as Moses was intended to be (in Christ). He saw David as David was intended to be. He saw Israel as Israel was intended to be. God saw 33 years of perfect righteousness, of obedience to the covenant. The human race in the person of Jesus was faithful as never before. So when He looked upon Israel that Sunday morning, He could only say, "Well done, good and faithful servant." The tomb could not hold such perfect righteousness, and Jesus came forth.

Acts 13:32, 33 well states the universal nature of the Resurrection: "We tell you the good news: What God promised our fathers he has fulfilled for us, their children, by raising up Jesus." God fulfilled His promises to us by raising up Jesus? At first glance that may puzzle us. But in light of all we have covered in this book, it should make sense now. God's promises are all about the covenant. Everything that He promised to His faithful Israel we find listed in Deuteronomy 28. And all of those things were fulfilled to us when God raised Jesus from the dead. Because Jesus represented the whole human race.

So at the cross the end-time judgment of the whole human race took place in the person of Jesus Christ. But doesn't the Bible also talk about a time when God will judge everyone in the whole world? How does that relate to the cross? To answer that we need to look at a few more texts. The judgment at the cross doesn't end there, but continues in the preaching of the gospel. John 3:18-21: "Whoever believes in him is not condemned, but whoever does not believe stands condemned already because he has not believed in the name of God's one and only Son. This is the verdict: Light has come into the world, but men loved darkness instead of light because their deeds were evil. Everyone who does evil hates the light, and will not come into the light for fear that his deeds will be exposed. But whoever lives by the truth comes into the light, so that it may be seen plainly that what he has done has been done through God." In this passage Jesus is the light that has come into the world. But wherever the light of Jesus goes judgment then takes place. By their actions people place themselves for Jesus or against Him.

John 5:24, 25 states essentially the same thing. Judgment didn't end at the cross, but continues every time someone preaches the gospel. Why? Because the gospel tells what Jesus Christ did—how on the cross the entire human race, including you and me, were

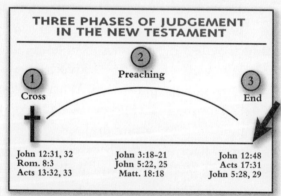

judged. If you accept Jesus Christ, then you embrace both aspects of that judgment. You receive both the condemnation on your own history and the approval of His perfect history. We could call this the second phase of judgment. The first phase involves the judgment of the whole human race at the cross. The second phase is the individual response to the judgment at the cross whenever someone presents the message of the cross.

Phase three of the judgment again involves the entire human race. But the final judgment is not different in character, nor is it some kind of double jeopardy. Basically, judgment number three simply asks each of us a question: "When you were confronted by judgment number two, what was your decision?" The final judgment at the end of the world does not present any other verdict than the one we render on ourselves in phase two. It just looks at the evidence of our decision and ratifies it for eternity.

Why go through all this trouble to understand the gospel? Because too often people attend a worship service or a Christian concert and leave having experienced God, but 24 hours later they have forgotten all about it. A relationship with God has to be more than just a good feeling. Feelings come and go. A relationship with God must have a solid infrastructure of Scripture and accurate information.

I have written this book because I want you to be a different person not only now, but two, three, four years from now. And that can happen only if you build your understanding upon a clear and compelling biblical foundation. It won't happen because you had an emotional high for three minutes yesterday or two weeks ago.

In order for me to have stability in my relationship with God I need to know that my standing with Him does not rest on vindictive wrath or impulsive love. If God's impulsive love saves me today, then I am in big trouble tomorrow, because I know you can't count on impulsive love. I have three kids, and I know something about impulsive love. "Daddy, I love you so much." And then two minutes later they do the very thing that you had warned them not to do. And of course this works the other way too. If our impulsive love for God is the basis for our salvation, we are in just as much trouble as if God Himself were impulsive.

The legal aspects of salvation are extremely important, because they assure us that the peace made by the cross is a lasting one. It is not something that is up and down, based on God's whim or my faithfulness. God doesn't change His method of operation whenever He feels like it. The stability of the legal language provides genuine security. In this legal language God binds Himself to the covenant that saves us. It is as if He says, "I am committed to your salvation. I'm not wavering, I'm not impulsive, I'm not vindictive."

A country ruled by a dictator instead of law has no security. You never know when the knock on the door is for you. You could be the dictator's brother or sister, brother-in-law or sister-in-law, or even son or daughter, but if you are in the way of the dictator, it's over. Unless a government operates on rule of law, nothing is secure and stable. Our God subjects Himself to the rule of law so we can know exactly where we stand and how He will behave toward us.

You won't find two versions of the gospel in the Bible. Both the Old and New Testaments teach that salvation results only from a mighty act of God. It never comes through the instability of human intentions. God fully vindicated His righteousness by what Christ did on the cross.

Now we are ready to unpack the full implications of this biblical picture. In the final section of this book we will build on the infrastructure of Scripture to lay out the basics of Christianity 101: how to get right with God and how to stay right with Him, how to have a relationship with God that doesn't come and go with the wind and the weather. The framework has been built, the big picture has been painted, and now it's time to apply the message of Scripture to today.

PART THREE

THE BIBLE
AND
EVERYDAY EXPERIENCE

CHAPTER 9

A NEW HISTORY

A TALE OF TWO HISTORIES

In this chapter we begin to look at the practical implications of the Bible's approach to putting God first. According to Scripture, everyone on earth needs a new history. Your history and my history are rooted in Adam. And what kind of background is that? It's a record of failure and disgrace. You can whitewash it or polish it up, but it is still embarrassing and disgraceful. And other people usually know that, no matter how cool you try to act.

I remember a situation that happened when I was about 17. A singing group came to my high school from a college that I was interested in. The woman who directed the group had a Ph.D. in music. But the singing group didn't impress me. I didn't think they were all that great. Later I stood by the drinking fountain discussing how Ph.D.s often lose touch with real life and how the director wasn't all that hot and so forth. Then I turned away from the drinking fountain to discover her standing right behind me. If you can relate to that—and I suspect you can—your history is just as disgraceful as mine.

When we look at things from the perspective of the Bible we learn that the whole of biblical history is our own personal history as well. First Corinthians 10:1, 2: "For I do not want you to be ignorant of the fact, brothers, that our forefathers were all under the cloud and that they all passed through the sea. They were all baptized into Moses in the cloud and in the sea." Although Paul was writing to the Corinthians, who were mostly Gentiles, he speaks about "our forefathers." Our history is rooted in Moses and the

Exodus. And that means it's also rooted in Adam and David—in failure and in disgrace.

The story of Old Testament Israel is your story and mine. It's a narrative of unfaithfulness. Much of the Old Testament is rated R, and there is a reason for that. It tells the tale of the human condition through the one people that might have had reason to boast that they were faithful to God. In the sex and violence of the Bible we see sin's destructiveness and the consequences of following a path of evil. The Old Testament is the record of your spiritual ancestors and mine. And it's a tale of failure and disgrace.

The good news, though, is that Jesus Christ went over that ground and redeemed it. The stories of the Bible are really about us. Everything Jesus did and said is really about us. When we realize that Jesus purposefully and intentionally lived out the experience of each of those Old Testament characters, we suddenly grasp the fact that He is the most important reality in the world. Everything that anyone has ever done is summed up in Him and in His experience. Just as our history is rooted in Adam, so it also is rooted in Jesus Christ.

Second Corinthians 5 is very clear on this. It reminds us that something about the mighty act of God in Jesus Christ affects everyone that lives or who ever lived. Second Corinthians 5:14, 15: "For Christ's love compels us, because we are convinced that one died for all, and therefore all died. And he died for all, that those who live should no longer live for themselves but for him who died for them and was raised again." Think back on everything we have covered in this book so far. Because Jesus Christ represents the entire human race, the entire human race in reality died with Him there on the cross.

"And he died for all, that those who live should no longer live for themselves but for him." By nature we all live for ourselves. We do everything possible to carry on our history, our legacy. But when we get a new legacy—a new history—we now live for the One who made that replacement history. If you get a new history in Jesus Christ, you do not have to live for your history anymore. Nor do you have to cover up for those mistakes. No longer do you have to hide them, keep secrets, or all the rest of that. Your old history is no longer a part of you, no longer threatens you.

Verse 17: "Therefore, if anyone is in Christ, he is a new creation; the old has gone, the new has come!" Do you remember how the New Testament sees Jesus as a new Creation? Christ sums up the entire Old Testament, bringing everything together at the cross. But Paul extends the concept to all of us. In Christ we reap that whole history, including His undoing of Old Testament history. When we identify ourselves with Him, we become a new creation ourselves. In Jesus Christ all of us have an alternative history, a totally different way of looking at reality, one filled with transforming power.

The Power of History

Why is this so important? Because our history tends to program both our present and our future. Let me give you an example. The phrase "digital divide" recognizes that if you live in an inner city "ghetto," or in a rural area that does not have reliable Internet access, you are likely to be much less familiar with the latest technology. What has happened to you in the past determines who you are and what you can yet become.

Some kids growing up today are computer saturated by the time they are 13. Others have never touched a keyboard. And if knowledge of technology is the key to the best jobs in the next generation, many children find themselves being preprogrammed for either success or failure. There will be children—Black, White, Hispanic, and Asian—who because of where they were born will be shaped for a different destiny than those who may live only 10 miles away. According to the Bible, every one of us has a history that determines what we are today. We can't just act as if it wasn't there. The powerful message of the New Testament is that in Jesus Christ God offers us an alternative history. We have a choice—we can take a history that was not ours and then apply it to ourselves.

When you are raised on computers, you are a different kid than one who is not. Or if you were raised in the ghetto, you have different hopes, different dreams, different aspirations than if you grew up in Buckingham Palace. Where you were raised and how you were raised determine a lot about your future. But in Jesus Christ we all have access to an alternative history. We all have the chance to become a child of the King. That changes everything. If you know that you are the child of the King, your thoughts are different, your hopes and dreams are different, your plans are different, and your actions are different. You live in the light of a special legacy.

The usual path to change is to try to become what you are not. The Bible calls this "works righteousness." "I'm going to be good today, not like yesterday," you tell yourself. The New Testament path to change, on the other hand, rests on the concept "Become what you are." It is recognizing who you are that changes you. When your defining history has changed, when you see Christ overruling your history, you realize that you can become a different person than you were before. You can become what you are!

History and Addiction

Most child abusers were abused children first. The majority of alcoholics have a history of alcohol use somewhere in the family. It's a vicious cycle from generation to generation. And it is the root of addiction. We become what we already are. Our family history programs us. And the mistakes that our parents made not only affect us, we pass them on to future generations.

If you go to a counselor who deals with addictions and ask for the key to positive change, the ultimate answer will be something like this: "You've got to break the chain enslaving the generations and stop the cycle of addiction. To make any permanent difference you've got to sever the link between your past and your future. If you don't do that, you are doomed to be just like your parents." Does something inside of you say, "No way! I'm not like my parents!" In one sense you're right, but in another you're wrong. Let's take a closer look at the generational pattern of addiction.

Imagine that in the first generation the father is an alcoholic. He arrives home at night screaming drunk, bangs through the door, and crashes facedown on the floor. On good days that is the last you hear from him until morning. The bad days are when he comes home awake and starts beating up your mother. And when he finishes with her he takes it out on you. What would go through your mind as a little child? *I will never be like my father. I will never do that.* And in one sense that child is probably right.

The problem is that while an alcoholic family has plenty of hatred for alcohol, the addiction itself nevertheless gets passed on. You grow up with the desperate need for some way to set your life straight, to feel like a person, to balance the pain with some pleasure. So in the next generation that child who will never be like his father may develop a sexual addiction of some kind. The addiction, pain, and anger are still there, but the drive to feel better now expresses itself in a different way.

In the case of sexual addiction the family members might gratify the sexual drive outside the home through prostitution or affairs, but all too often it may get dealt with inside the home through pornography or even sexual abuse. How do the children feel when they see the consequences that affairs, pornography, and sexual abuse bring into the home? It devastates them. And what do they say to themselves? "I will never be like my father [or mother, or both]!" And they too will be partly right.

So now you come to the third generation. By this time the family members may be sick of alcohol, sexual abuse, and so forth. So they manage to bottle up their drives and "do the right thing" by sheer force of will, but the addiction is still there. The chain remains unbroken. Members of the third generation may express themselves through anger instead. The father and the mother rage at each other or at the kids. They are addicted to anger. And what are the kids saying? "I will never be like that! Ever!"

Do you know what often happens in the third or fourth generation? "I will never be like my great-grandfather. I will never be like my grandpa. I will never be like my father." Time and again I have found that the fourth generation ends up going into ministry or one of the other helping professions. *I don't know how to solve the troubles in my life,* the thinking goes, *but maybe if I go into ministry (or become a counselor, a doctor, a social worker), I will be forced to become a good person. Perhaps in the process of rescuing others I can find healing for myself.* But it turns out that religion and psychology are not the answer either. Abuse and addiction can be even more damaging when clothed in the natural credibility of religious or professional garb.

I realize it is painful to even mention such things, but knowledge is power. You have to know you are hurt before you can be healed. Jesus said, "I did not come for the healthy; I came for those who are sick." If you do not know you are sick, you are probably not going to go to the doctor. You will spend your life running away from something deep down inside that you can't fix. That's the chain of abuse and dysfunction.

The New History

The only way to break this generational cycle is through a new history. To sever the chains that bind you, you must cease to be a child of your father and mother and now become a child of God through Jesus Christ. His perfect history becomes your inheritance, straight down from heaven. And from now on you run the race of life with your eyes fixed upon Him (Heb. 12:1, 2).

Paul understood exactly what I am talking about. Notice how he expressed it in Philippians 3:3-10. It is a long passage, but I want you to see it in its full context. Also I will intersperse brief comments in brackets. "For it is we who are the circumcision, we who worship by the Spirit of God, who glory in Christ Jesus, and who put no confidence in the flesh—though I myself have reasons for such confidence [Paul actually had a pretty good history, but keep reading]. If anyone else thinks he has reasons to put confidence in the flesh, I have more: circumcised on the eighth day [proud of it], of the people of Israel, of the tribe of Benjamin [a terrible heritage history—

check out Judges 19-21], a Hebrew of Hebrews [awesome]; in regard to the law, a Pharisee [very good]; as for zeal, persecuting the church [can't top that]; as for legalistic righteousness, faultless [wow, give me a piece of that history]. But whatever was to my profit I now consider loss for the sake of Christ [maybe coming to Jesus is hardest for people who are pretty good, and Paul was such a person]. What is more, I consider everything a loss compared to the surpassing greatness of knowing Christ Jesus my Lord, for whose sake I have lost all things. I consider them rubbish, that I may gain Christ and be found in him, not having a righteousness of my own that comes from the law, but that which is through faith in Christ—the righteousness that comes from God and is by faith. I want to know Christ and the power of his resurrection."

Paul clearly teaches the concept of two histories here: the old and the new. And no matter how good the old history was, you still have to walk away from it, because the new history is much, much better. It has life-changing power—the power of Jesus' resurrection. No other way exists to break the power of the past. The crucial question is "How do you do this? How do you take hold of the new history?" Paul speaks directly to the point in Romans 6:3-14.

Verses 3-7: "Or don't you know that all of us who were baptized into Christ Jesus were baptized into his death? We were therefore buried with him through baptism into death in order that, just as Christ was raised from the dead through the glory of the Father, we too may live a new life. If we have been united with him in his death, we will certainly also be united with him in his resurrection. For we know that our old self was crucified with him so that the body of sin might be done away with, that we should no longer be slaves to sin—because anyone who has died has been freed from sin."

Paul here takes the cosmic, universal event that happened at the cross and applies it to everyday life. This is the transition we also have to make as we apply the gospel to our everyday existence. The apostle says that the way to be free from sin—to escape the old history and the old ways—is to die (baptism is the physical illustration of this for him). You get rid of the old history by dying to it. The way to snap the chains binding us with the past is to bury the old history and live on the basis of the new one. But how do you do that in everyday experience? How can you die for real and at the same time live a new life? It is critical that we grasp the key to this paradox of the New Testament experience with Jesus.

Verse 8: "Now if we died with Christ, we believe that we will also live with him." Notice that his statement has two aspects: something is dead and something else comes alive. That's what this new history is all about. The chain to our past history shatters, and our relationship with Christ activates the new history. But perhaps you are thinking, *I thought I did that years ago. I tried that, I've been there, I accepted Jesus Christ—yet I'm still struggling with this stuff.* If that thought flashes through your mind, Paul hasn't overlooked you (see verse 11).

Verse 11: "In the same way, count yourselves dead to sin but alive to God in Christ Jesus." Sometimes we accept the new history we have in Christ and walk away from the old one. We think it is all buried and done with. And then the old man [or old woman] pops up out of the grave and starts running our life all over again. Maybe that happens off and on for you every day. What does Paul suggest you do then? Shove him or her back in the grave. How? By "counting yourself" dead to sin all over again.

Verses 12-14: "Therefore do not let sin reign in your mortal body so that you obey its evil desires. Do not offer the parts of your body to sin, as instruments of wickedness, but rather offer yourselves to God, as those who have been brought from death to life; and offer the parts of your body to him as instruments of righteousness. For sin shall not be your master, because you are not under law, but under grace."

Here is one of the most fantastic, most powerful passages in all the Bible. Paul declares that if sin is your master, you can't change your history. The shame and the condemnation of the law trap you. When you feel put down or rejected, every fiber of your being longs to feel better, longs to have a sense of worth. To alter the mood you may reach for chocolate, for alcohol, for a cigarette, or even a sexual plaything. But when you finish with your "medication" you still realize that nothing has changed. The sense of failure and inadequacy still remains.

But if you are under grace, you have a new history in Jesus Christ. At the ultimate center of everything that matters, you are accepted—you are OK—regardless of where you have been or what you have done. God's grace and acceptance become a mighty work in you that lifts you up and gives you a fresh start every day. Not because you deserve it, but because God, in His grace, provided it for you in Jesus Christ. It is a divine act just as mighty as the Exodus. And like the Israelites at the Red Sea, you don't have to earn it. When you make mistakes, when the old history rears up its head inside, you can "count yourself" once again dead to sin and alive in Christ. If a part of your body reaches out to do the wrong thing, you can offer that part of your body to God each day. Sin will not be your master when you are living in God's grace daily. Although you continue to have daily battles to fight, the new history overcomes the old history.

Do you remember the law of Deuteronomy? Obey and live, disobey and die. God respected that law when He sent Jesus. But notice the wonderful thing He has done. Through a mighty act of God an incredible reversal takes place. We have disobeyed, but Jesus Christ has obeyed. Jesus Christ obeys where we failed and then He dies, taking on Himself the curse we deserve. And so His obedience and His death produce life for those who have broken His commands. That is the incredible exchange of histories. He took your history and my history. Christ is the Second Adam, the second David, the second Moses. And He is also the second Paulien, having lived and redeemed my history. As a result I am free to walk in newness of life.

Notice this beautiful statement from the pen of Ellen G. White, a favorite author of mine. "Christ was treated as we deserve, that we might be treated as He deserves. He was condemned for our sins, in which He had no share, that we might be justified by His righteousness, in which we had no share. He suffered the death which was ours, that we might receive the life which was His" (*The Desire of Ages,* p. 25).

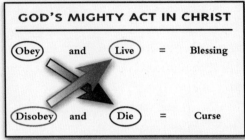

As we think about this great reversal, a question comes to mind. How is it possible for one person to die and enable all others to go free? It doesn't seem like an even—or even fair—match somehow. But follow me for a moment. Who is greater, an artist or his or her art? The artist, of course. Why? Because the work of art was in the artist's mind long before he or she formed it from stone or on canvas. Destroy the art piece, and the artist could produce another.

This realization was brought home to me about 1970 when a fellow wandered into Saint Peter's Basilica in Rome with a hammer under his jacket. He headed straight for Michelangelo's *Pietà,* which some consider the greatest piece of sculpture ever created. It is a magnificent image of Mary holding Jesus in her arms after He died on the cross. The man used his hammer to begin smashing that incredible sculpture apart. After guards wrestled him to the ground and hustled him off to jail, the authorities called in the greatest artists of Italy to put the statue back together again. After several weeks of careful work the head of that group of sculptors broke down in tears one day and said, "If only Michelangelo were here. He would know what to do."

You see, a piece of art existed in the artist's mind before anyone ever set it in stone or put it on canvas. The artist is truly greater than the art. This leads me to a second question. Who is greater, the Creator or the creation? The Creator, of course. Jesus is greater than the entire universe. Why? Because He made it all. The Gospel of John tells us that not a single thing came into existence apart from Him (John 1:3).

That means that Jesus Himself, the very one who died on the cross, is more than equal in value to the entire universe. Do you begin to see the worth of the cross? When Jesus died on the cross His death matched in value the loss of the entire universe. It equaled in value every sin ever committed or that ever could be committed. Christ's death on the cross provided a full and complete atonement for the entire universe. That is infinite value.

And when you see the tender care with which Jesus handled children and the outcasts of society—when you read the parable of the lost sheep—you realize that Jesus would have chosen to die even if it were just for you or me. That means that the cross assigns infinite value to every human being. And it is that kind of awareness that breaks the back of addiction and dysfunction. We will explore this sense of value more deeply in the next chapter.

CHAPTER 10

A NEW RELATIONSHIP WITH GOD

When I was a senior in high school things were going pretty well for me. The captain and the quarterback of a football team, I could throw fairly well, and the team could roll up some big scores. There was only one problem. In that league the captains of those teams not playing had to referee the other games. That's OK up to a point, but one day everything went wrong. I refereed a game observed by a spectator who was my personal hero. A teacher, a friend, and a man of God, he was the model of everything I wanted to be. Unfortunately for me, he had a strong interest in the outcome of the match.

The game hadn't gone on long before I could hear his voice. "That was a dumb call! What's the matter? Are you blind or something?" Time and again he had something to say about the quality of my refereeing. I tried my best to ignore him, but the impact of the comments began to pile up as the game went on. "Oh, come on; that was obvious! Are you asleep on your feet? I have never seen such a ridiculous display of refereeing in my whole life!"

I thought I was handling it adequately until that power sweep in the third quarter. The play ended up at the sideline, right in front of where he was standing. I was right on top of the play and did my best to make the correct call. "I don't believe it!" the man shouted. "I'm standing right here. I'm looking right at it. Are you stupid? Are you blind? What is your problem?" I turned to him and with trembling in my voice said, "Look, I'm doing the best I can."

He stared me right in the eye, paused for a couple of seconds, and then said with disgust in his voice, *"Your* best isn't good enough!"

We played that game in a little field in the middle of a major city. I picked up the football and in fury threw the greatest spiral of my life. It landed on the top of a three-story building across the street. Then I walked off the field with my head down. Finding the deepest and darkest corner of the basement in that school, I cried for two solid hours. Some of my teammates followed me down to the basement to offer their support, but it didn't help. I cried and I cried, and no one could stop me.

Why would a big, tough kid like me cry in front of his friends for two hours? It had to do with self-esteem, or self-worth—how I felt about myself deep down inside. The person that I admired most in my life thought that *my best wasn't good enough.* A little voice deep inside of me taunted, "Your best will *NEVER* be good enough. Your life is over. You're a failure. You'll never amount to anything."

Self-worth, whether we like it or not, is vital to the kind of life we live. How we feel about ourselves largely determines how we treat other people and how we face life's major issues. The search for a solid sense of what we are worth, therefore, is at the center of our quest for the best that life can offer. We will come back to this issue a little later.

THE LIMITS OF GOD'S MERCY

In the previous chapter we explored some of the implications of biblical history for our lives today. Now I would like to turn more directly to the legal aspects of how a person gets right with God and stays right with Him. To me this next concept is life and death for spiritual stability. You see, most types of Christian faith are grounded in the concept of the love and mercy of God, and they are certainly beautiful things. But a problem remains. Deep down inside of them most human beings have a sense that God's mercy will someday run out. Divine mercy has its limits—not because God's love has its limits, but there simply comes a point when mercy is no longer the appropriate response to evil. So to talk about the mercy of God, as true and right as that is, is not likely to provide a strong foundation for spiritual security.

In my own spiritual tradition we have seen an increased emphasis on God's love in recent years. And that has been needed. Yet it hasn't had the power and effect that people thought it would have. Somehow it hasn't resulted in changed lives the way we assumed it would. Preaching the love of God to somebody emotionally impaired doesn't work. Such people just say to themselves, "Well, God can love me all He wants, but I don't deserve it. And I just know the day is coming when He is going to say, 'You miserable wretch, I went to all the trouble of dying for you, I have put up with you all this time, now I've had enough.'"

So presenting God's love and mercy has its merits, but I have found that people are highly skilled at deflecting the significance of God's love in their minds. I believe we need to go deeper to provide people with spiritual security and stability. And that is to base our relationship with God on the legal characteristics of Scripture. It's not so much God's love as His justice that provides stability.

God Is Always Fair

You see, if you read the Bible carefully there is one thing you will never do, and that is to question that God's justice is not eternal. Will there ever be a day when He ceases to be fair? When God stops being just? No. In fact, that's often the thing about God we fear the most. "One of these days I'm going to get what I really deserve." So we dread divine justice even though it is that very justice of God that provides our greatest security in salvation. Let me explain how this works.

Would it be fair for any penal system to execute a person twice for the same murder (assuming that were somehow an option)? No. Remember what happened when Jesus died on the cross. Heaven placed all the sins of the human race on Him there. When Jesus perished at Calvary His death fully atoned for your sins and for mine. The cross broke the chains of sin and dysfunction. If your sins are atoned for in Jesus Christ, if He exhausted the curses of the covenant, if He died as the Second Adam, the new Israel, the new Moses—then that means that your sin has already been taken care of.

Yes, we can reject God's mighty act in Jesus Christ—we can say no to the cross. We can resist the gospel whenever preached to us. And if we do so, God allows us the freedom to go our own way. But we will end up making our own atonement in what the Bible calls the second death. Either way, the sin will be cared for. Yet we do not really need to endure the consequences of our sin—the second death—because it has already happened in Christ. It is not up to us whether or not our sins will be atoned for—they will be. Our choice is: how it will happen.

The legal books will be balanced in the end, one way or the other. But, you see, that would not be the case if someone who accepts Jesus then goes on to suffer the ultimate consequence of sin. That would be eternally unfair. The security of my salvation is not grounded in anything I do, thank God. Because the deeper I look into myself, the closer I examine my inner motives and all, the more I realize that I'm in big trouble—big, big, big trouble if I have to rely on myself.

The security of our relationship with God, thankfully, has its basis in a divine act of God. How much did Israel do to get out of Egypt? How far could they have gotten without His help? Yes, in the end they had to walk. They needed to accept what God had done and respond with their feet. But it was a mighty act of God that made the Exodus possible. You can't manufacture a relationship with God. In the end, a relationship with Him begins with something God has already done. And with our relationship with God grounded in His faithfulness, rather than our own, we can have real security.

This is vital at the practical level. People need to know that God won't suddenly turn on them for no reason. The fact of the matter is that if you are in Jesus Christ, God can't touch you. Now that's not the nicest way to put it, but it is the form many people need to hear. Some people are so afraid of God that they want some protection from Him before they can feel secure in their salvation. When abandonment and abuse have shattered your sense of trust and security, the thought of accepting God can be an extremely frightening thing!

The Search for Self-worth

If salvation provides no sense of security, however, our lives can never experience any lasting change. Consciously or unconsciously we will find a way to sabotage what God is trying to do for us. You want to know why? It is because every single one of us is searching for value. Every one of us has a need to feel like somebody, a need to be valuable. And if you don't find it in Jesus Christ, you will seek it somewhere else.

Let me show you how this works. First, let's discuss the search for self-worth. When people start looking for value in their lives they often begin with their possessions. They find their bottom line in bank accounts, in houses, or in cars. I remember a teenager named Chester, who grew up in the South Bronx, a run-down section of New York City. Once I asked him what he thought happiness was, and he exclaimed, "Happiness is a BIG, BLACK, CA-DEE-LAC." He was referring to the kind of car that the cool dudes in the hood—the pimps and the drug dealers—were driving. That's the bottom-line approach. He saw life's value in the fancy suits and slick cars of those considered "successful" in that neighborhood. Sometimes the only difference between the men and the boys is the price of their toys!

So you know what the problem is with this approach to self-worth? It doesn't last. Things scratch. They rot. They rust. They crash. Or the manufacturer comes out with a better Cadillac or BMW next year. Not only that, if you could have everything you wanted, it wouldn't be worth much to you anymore. What could you possibly give Bill Gates for Christmas? The more you have, the less valuable any individual thing seems. So *things* are not the answer to our need for worth. If you want a self-esteem, a self-worth that will last a lifetime, you're not going to find it in objects.

Not only do we have a relationship with the material world, we also have a relationship with ourselves. We may seek value in our performance, in our success. In this case it isn't the trappings of success (possessions) that turn us on, but the achievement itself that provides worth. "If only I could be like Michael Jordan or Tiger Woods," we tell ourselves, *"then* I would be somebody." Or "If only I could get a Ph.D. or become president of the company, then I'd be somebody. Perhaps if I looked like Brad Pitt or Julia Roberts, then I would be somebody."

But this kind of self-worth doesn't last either. When Michael Jordan began to hint about making a comeback at the age of 38, all the sportswriters started screaming, "Don't do it, Mike! We want to remember you the way you *were!* The high-flying slam dunks. The never-come-down floaters. It can't be like that anymore." The day comes when the body gets old. When Ph.Ds start losing their minds, and beauty queens become grandmas.

And even if you are on top of your game right now, you can still have a bad day. I remember the time I had just landed my dream job. I had a beautiful wife (still do), and a fat degree, and the students loved my classes. What more could I have wanted? Then I made four errors in a softball game and felt depressed for three days afterward. None of the successes cheered me up when I had a bad day. *A softball game?* you're saying to yourself. *Get a life, Paulien!* And you are absolutely right. I *do* have a life, but that day I fell into the performance trap, the idea that somehow I could find worth in my performance that would last for a lifetime. But it survived only until my next, albeit minor, failure. So, like the previous approach to self-worth, this one fails too.

So let's look at the third way people seek to find life, and that is through relationships with other people. We tend to value ourselves in terms of what other people think of us. If others regard us highly, we feel like someone of worth.

Have you ever seen teenagers fall in love for the first time? Suddenly the ugly duckling becomes a beautiful swan. The guy who stumbled over his tongue every time he walked out of the house now spouts Shakespeare. And the way they look at each other is wonderful to watch. What is happening? When other people value you it energizes your self-worth. That's why people like to drop names about celebrities. Because if some celebrity thinks highly of you, then you must *really* be somebody.

I'll never forget when I was 15 years old and the United States was having a presidential election. "Barry Goldwater is going to be speaking at the little airport about a mile from here," my older brother announced. "Let's go hear what he has to say." For those of you too young to remember, Barry Goldwater ran for president in 1964 and lost to Lyndon Johnson, who had taken over the presidency after the assassination of John F. Kennedy.

My brother parked the car, and we approached the airport hangar where the speech would take place. Suddenly three girls wearing red-white-and-blue Republican hats came running out of the building screaming, "He shook my hand! He shook my hand! I'll never wash it again!" Apparently they had gotten to meet the candidate and actually shook his hand. I have thought a lot about those girls since. I wonder what their hands look like today. At any rate, they certainly found a great deal of value in this now largely forgotten individual.

This source of self-worth, however, is no more stable than the first two. Celebrities, for one thing, are just as messed up as any of us—sometimes worse. And when we find a person who builds us up we enjoy it for a while and then discover that they have to move away, or perhaps they change their minds about us. Our sources of people-value can turn on us, betray us, divorce us, and even destroy us (think of the consequences of German devotion to Hitler). And even in the best of relationships, you have no guarantee that the person you love is going to be alive tomorrow.

If we could find the key to self-worth in money, in performance, and in relationships with other people, NBA basketball players would be the happiest people on earth. They have all of the above and then some. Yet professional basketball players have as high an incidence of drug and alcohol addiction as any other profession. It is painfully clear that the things we possess, what we have done, or the people we know do not provide reliable self-worth..

THE PATH TO SELF-WORTH

Fortunately, the story doesn't end there. There is hope and a way out. And it is this: if we could find the right kind of friend, a friend who has four specific qualities, it would make all the difference in the world. First, it would have to be somebody who is genuinely valuable. Somebody who is *really* worth something in their own right. The trouble with normal human relationships is that they involve flawed people who have reason to question their own worth. So the special relationship we have in mind requires a person of unique worth.

Second, this special friend would have to be somebody who knows everything there is to know about you. If a friend doesn't already know all about you, the next secret they stumble across might finish the relationship. You can have security only in a relationship that involves absolute transparency. You can then know that nothing you have done will threaten it, because the other person already knows everything. They already have enough evidence to make a permanent decision. The problem with human relationships is that they are ever evolving, and most people have great skill at hiding their true selves.

The third quality of the ideal friend is that, even though they know everything there is to know about you, they still love you just the way you are. The relationship does not depend on your performance. And, finally, that friend has to be somebody who never dies, because death always threatens even the perfect relationship. Does such a friend exist? Or are we just losing ourselves in fantasy here?

If such a friend were to exist, however, it would make all the difference in the world. It would give us a self-worth that never changes. We wouldn't have to suffer the constant ups and downs that afflict us in our regular relationships. Such a friend would enable us to have inner peace, allowing us to come to the place where it really wouldn't matter what others thought about us. A relationship like that would bring a sense of genuine fulfillment in life. And the fascinating thing is that when your personal needs are met, it frees you to meet the needs of others without expecting anything in return. You don't have to get paid for what you do or perform. No longer do you have to "fix the whole universe" in order to feel as if what you do matters.

I have incredibly good news for you. The Bible we have been studying together makes it perfectly clear that such a unique friend exists. His name is Jesus Christ. He possesses all the four qualities that we need. He is worth the entire universe, because He made it all. He is all-knowing, which means He knows everything about us. In spite of that knowledge, however, the cross demonstrates that He loves each of us just the way we are. We don't have to earn His favor by achievement or success. And, finally, the Bible teaches that the One who died and rose again has broken the chains of death. He will never die again. And He offers a "forever friendship" to every one of us.

There is nothing wrong with money, with achievements, or with having relationships with other people. These three things are the sum and substance of life as we know it on earth. But in Jesus Christ my self-worth does not depend on how much I earn or how many students choose to take my class. Nor does it rest on whether or not my teenagers turn out just the way I would like. And if my self-worth is thoroughly grounded in that upward relationship with God, then I no longer have to worry about what other people think of me. I will be free to serve others and to make a difference in this world. I can love because I am loved. I can forgive because I am forgiven. And I can show mercy to the erring and the troubled because I have already received it myself.

It seems to me that this insight about Jesus explains why Christianity has flourished for 2,000 years despite the many efforts to stamp it out. It explains the martyrs of the Christian faith, who chose to die rather than give up Jesus. Such a choice makes sense only when one has gained so much from a relationship that life would not be worth living without it.

I believe this insight about Jesus also helps us understand what sin and temptation are all about. There is such a thing as gross evil. But most people don't find themselves tempted to do those kinds of acts. Most people struggle with good things. It is often the good things that occupy our time and distract us from the ultimate thing, our relationship with Jesus Christ. We all gather possessions, know some people, and do some good things. But when our need for self-worth lets those things draw us away from God, that is temptation.

So the next time you feel a strong craving for possessions, performance, or people, ask yourself some questions. Will this new toy help me to glorify God? Will it enhance my relationship with God or distract me from it? Why do I feel that I need to go back to school and get this degree? Is it to make a difference in the world for God, or is it because I am not meeting my deepest needs in Christ? Why am I finding this member of the opposite sex so attractive? Is whatever this is a path to real fulfillment or just another dead-end way to satisfy needs apart from a relationship with Jesus Christ?

Possessions, performance, and people are fundamental aspects of life. In their proper place their pursuit is spiritually and emotionally healthy. But being right with God is the one thing that really matters. We can find true and lasting self-worth only in a relationship with God. Unless we have grounded our possessions, our performance, and our relationships in a living relationship with God, they will eventually lead to great disappointment or even destruction.

I want to close this section with three Bible passages that speak very clearly to these matters. The first is Jeremiah 9:23, 24: "This is what the Lord says: 'Let not the wise man boast of his wisdom or the strong man boast of his strength or the rich man boast of his riches, but let him who boasts boast about this: that he understands and knows me, that I am the Lord, who exercises kindness, justice and righteousness on earth, for in these I delight,' declares the Lord." True life does not arise from riches, strength, or wisdom. Nor do we find it in possessions or performance. Only in the Lord we can safely boast.

John 12:42, 43: "Yet at the same time many even among the leaders believed in him. But because of the Pharisees they would not confess their faith for fear they would be put out of the synagogue; for they loved praise from men more than praise from God." Here we find out that many followers of Jesus failed to "come out of the closet" because they feared the loss of human relationships. They placed their relationships with fallible mortals ahead of the ultimate relationship.

Galatians 6:14: "May I never boast except in the cross of our Lord Jesus Christ, through which the world has been crucified to me, and I to the world." Here Paul summarizes the whole matter in a sentence. The "world" is all about possessions, performance, and people. They are a good and necessary part of our lives. But if they become the source of "boasting," the basis on which we measure our value, we must allow them to be crucified to us in Christ. When we come to Jesus, in one sense we lose the whole world, yet in another we gain it all and more. Once we have grounded our existence in Christ, life becomes truly worth living.

In the last chapter of this book we will look at the kind of life a person takes up when they have a relationship with God through the mighty act of Jesus Christ. What does it mean to be a follower of Jesus? How does that change the way we live from day to day?

CHAPTER 11

A NEW WAY TO LIVE

LIVING THE LIFE OF FAITH

In the previous two chapters we have seen how the historical and legal characteristics of the Bible provide a secure and stable basis for getting right with God. Our standing with God does not rest on our possessions or our performance, but is grounded in a mighty act of God, the cross of Jesus Christ. In that event Jesus not only created a perfect history to put in place of our imperfect one, but He exhausted the curses of the covenant that condemned us to death and frustration.

In Jesus Christ God frees us from the shackles of the past. He liberates us from the insecurities of depending on our own performance. We have a new history and a new relationship with God. Because we have grounded our lives on the mighty acts of God, it makes it possible for us not only to enter into a relationship with God but to live a completely new kind of life. Freed to love and to give, we now experience joy in helping others discover the security and stability that we have found in Christ.

This leads us to the concluding portion of this book. In the light of the mighty act of God in Christ, how shall we now live? What should be different in our lives? How can we place Christ at the center of all that we do, say, or think? How can we put into practice the new life that we have found? Paul summed up the new life in one short sentence: "For to me, to live is Christ and to die is gain" (Phil. 1:21).

How does Paul define our response to God's mighty deed in Christ? He says: "For to me, to live is Christ." Christ is somehow at the center of everything the apostle does and says and is. But how do you do this in practice? How do you make it real in everyday life? Paul does not bother defining that too clearly here. So we need to search a little bit further and ask the question of the whole Bible, "How do you *live Christ?*" What does it mean in practice?

We will find the biblical answer to these questions by returning one last time to the Old Testament and see how the saints of its time lived out their faith. Imagine yourself a neighbor of Ruth and Boaz back in ancient Bethlehem (read the romantic story of how they got together in the biblical book of Ruth). How was life different because they knew the God of Israel? What was the Old Testament life of faith really like?

The Story of Ruth and Boaz

Let's imagine that it is about 1100 B.C. in the town of Bethlehem during the era of the Judges. Ruth and Boaz have settled down after their happy wedding day. They are having children, farming their land, and living the life that God has given them. Let's suppose that one day a Babylonian merchant passes by on his way to Egypt. He is going to go down to Egypt to talk to some people he met there the last time and discuss ways to make lots of money together. Already he has been on his way for more than a month (800 miles on foot), but it's getting toward the end of the day and he stops for rest under the shade of a tree overlooking a little farm.

As he sits there he observes some people doing farmwork and notices that the field manager is treating them with respect. It surprises him, because his native Babylon regarded the average farm laborer as worthless scum. But the field manager is being kind to the workers, treating them as equals. Then he notices that the landowner has come over to the field manager and works with him as a colleague instead of as master and slave.

"This is weird," the Babylonian merchant tells himself. "I've never seen anything like this. I've got to find out what's behind this."

One of the laborers wanders close to where the Babylonian is resting, so he calls him over. "Hey, you got a minute?"

The worker looks him over as he approaches and notices that he is Babylonian by the style of his clothes. "Sure, you need some directions?"

"No, I think I'm OK. I've been by here before. I just have a question. I notice your boss treats you real nice. Is there any reason for that?"

"Well, this is an Israelite home," the laborer replies, "and we worship the Lord. You see, a long time ago we were wretched and hopeless slaves in the land of Egypt. But the Lord brought us out of there with a mighty hand and an outstretched arm. And He instructed us that from now on whenever we are in charge we should be kind to those who work for us, regardless of their status in society."

A little suspicious about the Israelite's explanation, the Babylonian asks to speak to the field manager and see what he has to say about it. When the field manager comes over he tells him, "I've been noticing how nice you are to your workers here. I'm not used to this. Can you tell me why you do it that way?"

"Well, it's like this. Long ago we were slaves in the land of Egypt. But the Lord our God brought us out from there with a mighty hand and an outstretched arm, so, you know, we might as well be nice to slaves, because we know what it feels like to be one."

"That's pretty cool. I like that. I wish people always treated me that way."

"Hey, would you like to meet Boaz?" the field manager asks. "He's the owner of the farm. You could learn more about it from him."

The merchant looks surprised. "He would talk to me, a Babylonian? Rich people don't talk to foreigners unless they have to."

"Well, I think this rich guy is different from what you're used to." The field manager motions Boaz over to where the Babylonian merchant has been resting under the tree.

Before the Babylonian can even say anything, Boaz says, "Welcome to Bethlehem," then glances at the setting sun. "You know, it's getting late. Why don't you spend the weekend with us?"

This is a little too much for the merchant. Maybe it is some kind of trap. For an instant he allows a look of rejection mingled with a little fear to cross his face.

"Hey, relax," Boaz says. "One of my field hands told me you are going all the way to Egypt. There's no need to rush off. Take a break, get yourself refreshed, and then in a couple days you can move on. Don't worry about it—we do this all the time."

"That's really cool. I appreciate it. Nothing like this ever happened to me in Egypt. Nor has anything like it ever happened to me in Syria. I just don't get it. How come you invited me, a total stranger? I could be a serial killer for all you know."

Boaz looks the Babylonian over briefly and grins. "I'll take my chances. Live dangerously, they say."

"How much will I need to pay?" the merchant asks.

For just an instant a shadow crosses Boaz's face. Is he just a little hurt by the stranger's question? Then he says evenly, "This is not about money. You won't owe us a thing. Actually there's something else behind all this. You see, a long time ago we were foreigners in the land of Egypt, but the Lord our God freely brought us out with a mighty hand and an outstretched arm. We received so much from Him that we've learned to enjoy doing things for people who can't pay us back, or just being hospitable to strangers. His kindness produces our kindness. Knowing Him is pay enough for one lifetime."

The Babylonian replies with an openness that startles him, "Man, I like this religion of yours. May I learn more about it this weekend?"

So the Babylonian merchant joins them at the main house. Since it happens to be Friday, the final Sabbath preparations are taking place. Ruth sets out oil lamps as the merchant walks in. As they gather for supper, he hears about the Sabbath for the first time.

"What's this about, this Sabbath business?" the visitor questions.

"Oh, one day a week we all take off from work and spend it worshiping the Lord and enjoying each other's company," Ruth explains.

"Whoa, time out!" the merchant interrupts. "You can't do that, I mean, think of all the money you are losing, taking a day off every week!"

"Well, that's what we do, and we seem to be doing all right."

The Babylonian glances around the well-appointed home and sees no point in arguing the issue. So he asks instead, "Why are you doing this? There must be some reason."

"Well, it's like this," Ruth responds. "We were slaves in the land of Egypt, and the Lord our God brought us out with a mighty hand and an outstretched arm. So He told us to keep the Sabbath, and not only us, but to allow all our workers the same privilege. So that's what we decided to do."

And the Babylonian thinks to himself, *What on earth is going on? This is getting real interesting.* Out loud he says, "I think I understand where you're coming from. Your God has saved you from a fate worse than death, and now you are living well, so I can appreciate the way you feel about Him. But why do you need to be so obsessed about this? You already have everything you need. Why do you focus everything on the past?"

"Yes, it's true," Ruth observes, "that we have worked hard to get where we are. And it's true that we are reasonably happy and successful. It would be easy to forget that God is behind all our success today. But every grape and every grain of wheat is just as much a miracle as our exodus from Egypt. We feel it would be dangerous to forget God in the middle of His daily gifts to us."

"That's right," Boaz adds. "By remembering the mighty things our Lord did for us in the past, we remember the mighty things He is doing for us today—the everyday things that are so easy to overlook. We've worked hard, but we still feel we owe everything to Him."

After dinner they gather contentedly around the fire. The merchant sprawls among some plush pillows and stares dreamily at the flames. Is his life somehow changing this day? Will things ever be the same? He can't remember when he has ever felt so happy or content.

After a while Ruth and Boaz start talking about the Passover feast scheduled the following week. They are planning to travel up to the sanctuary to celebrate.

"Why are you going to do that?" the Babylonian asks, then interrupts himself, "No, don't tell me! Let me guess. You were strangers in the land of Egypt, right?"

Ruth, Boaz, and the rest of the family explode with laughter. When things settle down, Boaz says to his wife with a grin, "I think he's got it!"

With an earnest look the merchant says hopefully, "Do you think I could go along? Would it be all right if I stayed the whole week? I want to know more about this deity of yours."

Ruth and Boaz seem delighted. "Of course it would be all right. Hey, you're a stranger in the land of Israel, and that means everything is all right with you. Be our guest. It will be fun."

Boaz and Ruth had learned that in every detail of life it is possible to remember what God has done. Each of us acts as if we had walked through the Red Sea and it had become our own personal history. That is what the Jewish Passover is all about. Jews gather around a table and say, *"We* were strangers in the land of Egypt." Not *they,* but *we.* "The Lord brought *us* out." Israel's everyday life was to continually remind them of God's acts for them.

The Old Testament Life of Faith

You see, Old Testament faith was God-centered, not human-centered. True faith does not focus so much on what we do, but on what God does. It's about putting Him first in our lives. That's the bottom line. Psalm 111:4: "He has caused his wonders to be remembered; the Lord is gracious and compassionate." What did it mean to remember God's mighty deed in Old Testament times, and what does that involve today?

Psalm 78:5-8: "He decreed statutes for Jacob and established the law in Israel, which he commanded our forefathers to teach their children, so the next generation would know them, even the children yet to be born, and they in turn would tell their children. Then they would put their trust in God and would not forget his deeds but would keep his commands. They would not be like their forefathers—a stubborn and rebellious generation, whose hearts were not loyal to God, whose spirits were not faithful to him."

Here we see the psalmist rehearsing the mighty acts of God in behalf of the patriarchs and at the Exodus. The bottom line of Old Testament faith was to keep God's wonderful deeds constantly on the spiritual radar screen. In Old Testament terms the proper response to the mighty acts of God was rehearsal—telling and retelling them. But that is a rather sweeping statement. What does rehearsal or retelling really involve in actual practice? I would like to suggest five different ways that the Old Testament saints rehearsed God's mighty acts. I could provide a number of texts to illustrate each of these, but I'll limit myself to one in most cases.

1. THROUGH VERBAL RECITAL

The most obvious way that the Old Testament saints rehearsed the mighty acts of God was to tell the story again and again. During worship services. At school. When walking from place to place. Sitting around the campfire. We find a great example in Deuteronomy 6:20-24: "In the future, when your son asks you, 'What is the meaning of the stipulations, decrees and laws the Lord our God has commanded you?' tell him: 'We were slaves of Pharaoh in Egypt, but the Lord brought us out of Egypt with a mighty hand. Before our eyes the Lord sent miraculous signs and wonders—great and terrible—upon Egypt and Pharaoh and his whole household. But he brought us out from there to bring us in and give us the land that he promised on oath to our forefathers. The Lord commanded us to obey all these decrees and to fear the Lord our God, so that we might always prosper and be kept alive, as is the case today.'" God invited them to memorialize the Exodus by constantly relating the story to their children and anyone else who would listen. Each Israelite was to be ready to recite it on a moment's notice. And the content of that story was the mighty acts of God.

2. Through the Sabbath and the Feast Days

Deuteronomy 5 offers a second look at the Ten Commandments, which first appear in Exodus 20. The fourth commandment, regarding the Sabbath, reads a bit differently here. "Remember that you were slaves in Egypt and that the Lord your God brought you out of there with a mighty hand and an outstretched arm. Therefore the Lord your God has commanded you to observe the Sabbath day" (Deut. 5:15).

Exodus 20 offers Creation as the basis for Sabbath observance, while Deuteronomy 5 urges Sabbath observance because God had brought Israel out of Egypt. The people were to remember the Sabbath day because they had been slaves in the land of Egypt. When they kept the Sabbath each week they were reminding themselves that they were no longer slaves. No longer did they have to work night and day. The Sabbath brought to their minds God's mighty deeds that had rescued them from perpetual slavery and kept them free to serve Him with gladness. So Sabbathkeeping was another way that people in Old Testament times rehearsed the mighty divine acts.

What was true of the Sabbath was also the case for the other feasts on the Israelite calendar. Passover celebrated the deliverance from Egypt recorded in Exodus 12. The Feast of Tabernacles memorialized the years they had lived in tents under God's protection. What I find fascinating is that archaeologists have discovered that the Canaanites observed annual feasts like those in the Bible before the Israelites ever reached Palestine. The Canaanites also followed an agricultural year. At planting time they would have a planting celebration. Then at harvest they would have a harvest celebration. To close the midsummer drought they would have a rain dance.

But a crucial difference existed between Canaanite worship and Israelite worship. For the Canaanites the agricultural feasts were simply an annual cycle that went on and on, simply a way to bring rain and enhance the fertility of the soil. What God did was turn these agricultural cycles into history lessons. The Israelites weren't now just going through an agricultural routine. They were remembering the mighty acts of God in their past. Each celebration remembered specific historical events. God, in a sense, sanctified these festivals with His mighty acts. They became rehearsals of what He had done.

3. Through Obedience

For the Israelites obedience was never something isolated in its own right—it always had its basis in God's mighty interventions, particularly the Exodus. Deuteronomy 11:1-8: "Love the Lord your God and keep his requirements, his decrees, his laws and his commands always. Remember today that your children were not the ones who saw and experienced the discipline of the Lord your God: his majesty, his mighty hand, his outstretched arm; the signs he performed and the things he did in the heart of Egypt, both to Pharaoh king of Egypt and to his whole country; what he did to the Egyptian army, to its horses and chariots, how he overwhelmed them with the waters of the Red Sea as they were pursuing you, and how the Lord brought lasting ruin on them. . . . But it was your own eyes that saw all these great things the Lord has done. Observe therefore all the commands I am giving you today, so that you may have the strength to go in and take over the land that you are crossing the Jordan to possess."

When Moses makes this proclamation Israel is on the other side of the Jordan River about to begin the conquest of Palestine. What are they supposed to do? They are to remember God's mighty acts in the past in order that they may have the strength to accomplish the new task that He has set before them (cf. also Ex. 20:2, 3 and Deut. 7:7-11).

Clearly in this passage the retelling of God's wondrous deeds is more than just verbal. It is summed up also in obedience to God's laws. And every act of obedience was to be in remembrance of what God had already done. Such obedience was never to be legalistic, but was always grounded in gratitude to God for what He had previously accomplished. Everything we do in obedience is to be in response to what He has already done.

4. Through Ethical Behavior

For ancient Israel the Exodus was the basis for all behavior. So the mighty acts of God also affected the way Israelites were supposed to treat people. Deuteronomy 10:19-22: "And you are to love those who are aliens, for you yourselves were aliens in Egypt. Fear the Lord your God and serve him. Hold fast to him and take your oaths in his name. He is your praise; he is your God, who performed for you those great and awesome wonders you saw with your own eyes. Your forefathers who went down into Egypt were seventy in all, and now the Lord your God has made you as numerous as the stars in the sky."

What is an alien? Well, back then they didn't have three eyes and antennae! An alien in Old Testament times was anyone who didn't come from your neighborhood. The Israelites themselves had been "aliens" in the land of Egypt. God now asks them to treat aliens and foreigners in the light of their own experience in Egypt. Notice verse 18: "He [God] defends the cause of the fatherless and the widow, and loves the alien." So they were to behave like God, who had rescued the aliens in the time of the Exodus. And if you know that God has brought you out from slavery with a mighty hand and an outstretched arm, the next time you run into a slave you are more likely to treat that person differently.

5. Through the Routines of Life

The Israelites were to keep the mighty acts of God in their consciousness throughout all the routines of life. Deuteronomy 26:1, 2: "When you have entered the land the Lord your God is giving you as an inheritance and have taken possession of it and settled in it, take some of the firstfruits of all that you produce from the soil of the land the Lord your God is giving you and put them in a basket. Then go to the place the Lord your God will choose as a dwelling for his Name."

God is saying here, "I want every aspect of your life to focus on the mighty acts that I have done for you. If you want to experience true life, you will think about Me when you plant your seed. When you are cultivating the soil your thoughts will dwell on Me. Later, when you are harvesting the crops, your thoughts will also be on Me." And to encourage them to do this in the daily routines of life, He even created a ceremony in which they were to take a basketful of the firstfruits of the harvest, bring them to the sanctuary, and recite the mighty acts of God.

But such meditation about God was to be no idle musing. Hebrew reminiscence was always full of action. When the Israelites remembered what God had done, they were to rehearse His deeds through their own words and actions. Now this is the really exciting part. When you rehearse the mighty acts of God, the power of God's original intervention energizes what you are doing in the present! The divine acts become real in your own experience.

One Old Testament passage unpacks this in detail: 2 Chronicles 20:1-23. It is a long text, so I'll offer only the highlights here, but I would encourage you to read the whole story for yourself. The Moabites, Ammonites, and Meunites have attacked Israel. It is three against one. If it were football it would be the ultimate blitz (the quarterback is dead). The enemy army has already crossed the Dead Sea (so much for natural barriers) and is less than 30 miles from Jerusalem. Israel faces a serious crisis.

Alarmed, King Jehoshaphat proclaims a fast for all Judah. From all over the nation people come to the Temple to pray to the Lord. Jehoshaphat gets up in front of the crowd to lead the prayers. Now if you were in his shoes, what would you pray about? "O Lord, help us, do something please! We're in big trouble!" Prayers get real focused when you are about to die! But Jehoshaphat's actual prayer doesn't sound desperate at all. Let's listen in: "O Lord, God of our fathers, are you not the God who is in heaven? You rule over all the kingdoms of the nations. Power and might are in your hand, and no one can withstand you. O our God, did you not drive out the inhabitants of this land before your people Israel and give it forever to the descendants of Abraham your friend? They have lived in it and have built in it a sanctuary for your Name, saying, 'If calamity comes upon us, whether the sword of judgment, or plague or famine, we will stand in your presence before this temple that bears your Name and will cry out to you in our distress, and you will hear us and save us'" (verses 6-9).

What is Judah's king doing here? He is rehearsing God's mighty acts from his past. He speaks confidently of God's promise to Solomon (1 Kings 8:22-53), just a few generations before, that if they ever got in trouble with an attacking army, they just needed to go to the Temple and rehearse the mighty acts of God. So Jehoshaphat was just following instructions. "But now here are men from Ammon, Moab and Mount Seir," he continued, "whose territory you would not allow Israel to invade when they came from Egypt; so they turned away from them and did not destroy them. See how they are repaying us by coming to drive us out of the possession you gave us as an inheritance. O our God, will you not judge them? For we have no power to face this vast army that is attacking us. We do not know what to do, but our eyes are upon you" (2 Chron. 20:10-12). Immediately a prophet of God stands up and tells them not to worry about the battle. They should go down to the battlefield and take their positions, but they won't have to fight. God will do it for them.

So how does Jehoshaphat respond? He sends out the Temple choir to lead the army into battle! He even orders the song they are to sing, one called, "Give Thanks to the Lord, for His Love Endures Forever." Verses 22, 23: "As they began to sing and praise, the Lord set ambushes against the men of Ammon and Moab and Mount Seir who were invading Judah, and they were defeated. The men of Ammon and Moab rose up against the men from Mount Seir to destroy and annihilate them. After they finished slaughtering the men from Seir, they helped to destroy one another."

The next time the United States is in danger, do you think the president will send a choir out to fight? Not likely. So what was the choir doing that day in Jerusalem? They were rehearsing the mighty acts of God. But they weren't singing "Trust and Obey." "Trust and

Obey" is a good song, but it wouldn't have been the right one on that day. Instead, they were singing, "Give Thanks to the Lord, for His Love Endures Forever." The people focused on God, not on their problem.

And what happened when they rehearsed the mighty acts of God in their past? The power of the original act—the power of the Exodus—manifested itself in their midst. The mighty act in the past became the focus of their lives in the present, and the result was even greater mighty acts to celebrate in the future! So for Old Testament Israel, all that God had done in the past became the focus of life in the present.

THE NEW TESTAMENT LIFE OF FAITH

The New Testament updates these concepts to the situation in which *we* find ourselves. Jesus Christ fulfills the entire life, experience, and history of the Old Testament and its people. All of Old Testament Israel's history and experience comes together in the Christ event—in Jesus Christ at the cross. And everything in the New 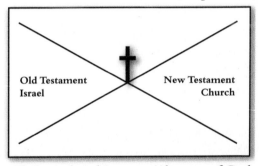 Testament era points back to Christ as the ultimate mighty act of God.

If Jesus Christ embodies Israel's entire history, that heritage becomes ours too when we are united to Him. We become part of that whole history, but it is a past that has already been redeemed through the life of Christ. It is now a beautiful history in Him. Just as Old Testament believers had their eyes focused on the Exodus, so New Testament believers keep their eyes centered on the cross, and in so doing they see the entire Old Testament in a fresh light.

For the New Testament the cross of Jesus Christ is *the* greatest and mightiest act of God. The cross sums up all the history and experience of the Old Testament. This is the greatest act God has ever done in behalf of His people. As Creator, His one death is sufficient to redeem the entire universe. And since it is sufficient, the only way it can be repeated is to retell what has already been done.

But what has God done for me personally? Are there mighty acts of God in my life too? First of all, as we saw a couple chapters ago, He has given me a new history. No longer who I once was, I have a new identity. I have received a fresh start in Jesus Christ. It is as if my whole past had never happened, as if it were washed away. And this new history makes a huge difference in the area of self-worth, in the realization of how much God values me.

Is that a mighty act of God? I think so. When a person spends decades wallowing in self-pity, mired in a sense of failure—of never being good enough—what could be mightier than an act that validates you as the most valuable person in the universe? Would it do something for your self-esteem if the president of the United States chose to be your friend? consulted your opinion on a regular basis? I think it would make a huge difference.

But compare the power of the president with that of Jesus Christ, who made the entire universe. Making the universe is a lot tougher than getting a tax bill passed. It's also far more significant. When the greatest person in the universe chooses to be your friend it places tremendous value upon you. So the mighty act of God for me is a new history, a new start, a new sense of what I am worth. And there is no greater miracle than that.

That's the historical side of God's mighty act for me, but it also has a legal aspect. As we saw in the previous chapter, I also have a new sense of being right with God, a new relationship with Him. Everyone has a sense of failure. All of us know that we are not living up to all that we know is right, that we are not "being all that we could be," as the United States Army puts it. So it is not enough just to have a new history. I need to know that my new history is legal, that it is acceptable to God. I must experience the security of being right with God.

Here we have the secret to a secure and stable faith, to the realization that our standing with God is grounded in an unassailable legal action. In the United States, when the Supreme Court says "You're free," nothing else in this country can change that. No police officer can alter that fact. You can drive by that police car with confidence and say, "You can't touch me, because the Supreme Court said so." Perhaps you notice a couple soldiers standing there with machine guns, looking threatening. Don't worry. With the authority of the Supreme Court you can tell them, "You can't touch me." That's the kind of security we can have in Christ.

So God has done mighty acts not just for us; He has done mighty acts for me. He has changed my whole life in tremendous ways, and one of the most exciting aspects is that I can lose the fear of death. I first realized this in Jerusalem in 1995, when I was walking down a street in the Muslim quarter of the old city. As I came around a corner, suddenly six screaming guys came charging at me. And the strangest thing happened—I just didn't react. I wasn't scared. I didn't run. It turned out to be my students playing a trick on me. They had seen me coming, so they hid and ambushed me. Quite upset afterward, they sputtered, "That was no fun. You didn't react—you weren't scared or anything."

How come I didn't react? I asked myself. *I didn't fake that. Something has happened here. Something is different.* Then I realized that something deep inside of me—something that I had no control over—did not feel threatened. That was totally awesome for me. There's something very real that happens when you know you are right with God. You may not notice it tomorrow. It may not happen next week or even next year, but one day it hits you that God has done a mighty act inside of you. The day comes when you wake up realizing that you are a different person. For some people the feeling may take years, but it will occur. And when it does, it is awesome—it is a mighty act. Master the teachings of the Bible, apply them every day, count yourself dead to sin and alive in Christ, and in His time He will make all the difference. This is the only path of life that really works. I know—I have tried a few.

What then? How do we live in the light of God's mighty acts for us? How can we celebrate the cross in the twenty-first century? Let me offer several ways that the New Testament suggests.

1. Through Sharing the Gospel

The Old Testament saints celebrated the mighty acts of God verbally. The New Testament equivalent of that verbal rehearsal is the gospel. What is the gospel? We find its New Testament definition in 1 Corinthians 15:1-8. According to Paul, the gospel in a nutshell is roughly, "Jesus coming to this earth, living a perfect life, dying on the cross, and being raised on the third day for us."

Now that never made sense to me before. How can the gospel be a simple series of events that happened 2,000 years ago? But I understand now. It is a mighty act of God. Sharing the gospel is simply letting people know that God has accomplished everything that needs to be done in order for them to become the kind of person they want to be. Proclaiming the gospel is telling and retelling the story of the mighty act of God in Jesus Christ. It is a mighty deed like the Exodus, the Creation, and all the other mighty events that we find in Scripture.

The exciting thing about sharing the gospel is that it is never dry; it is never simply an intellectual process. As you present it to others the Holy Spirit is present to press the claims of the gospel on the listener. As in 2 Chronicles 20, it brings the power of the original act into the present situation. What is the power of the cross? It is the Resurrection. Whatever your need might be today, it is nothing compared to raising someone from the dead!

But we receive still another added benefit when we share the gospel. The power of the Resurrection is not limited to the person you are talking to. When the Holy Spirit presses the claims of the cross as a result of our witness, we receive that power too. Sharing with others also brings us power. Whenever human beings tell and retell the mighty acts of God, it leads to spiritual revival and reformation. And it is God who does it, not a preacher or a teacher.

The lay leader of a large church felt his spiritual experience going dry. For whatever reason he couldn't connect with the preaching in his church. His walk with God was slipping away, and he was about ready to give up. But he decided to offer it one more chance. One Sunday morning he went down to the little Baptist church in town. Bad luck. The preacher was away that week, and the deacon was up there reading something or other. He was mumbling along, and the congregation was half asleep. *Good grief,* the man thought, *this is my last chance and this has to happen.* But a funny thing happened. Every 5 or 10 minutes the deacon, who seemed totally clueless, lifted his eyes from the reading and said, "Well, I don't know about that, but I do know one thing: God is able." Then he would again mumble on for 5 or 10 minutes and then repeat, "Well, I don't know about that point, but I do know this: God is able."

About 20 minutes into that sermon the elder began to sense God's presence warming his heart. Later he told me, "I just suddenly realized that God *is* able. God is able to take me where I am—it doesn't matter who is preaching." Nor does it matter how dead the church is or how out-of-date the worship service is. If you rehearse the mighty acts of God, He is able to resurrect the dead! In order to be effective, worship needs to be God-centered. It must be focused on the gospel—on what God has already done.

2. Through the Ceremonies of the Church

A second way we can rehearse the mighty acts of God in today's world is by performing the traditional ceremonies of the church just as God's people celebrated the feasts in ancient times. What are those special ceremonies? Some people suggest that in order to be a Christian one has to celebrate the festivals of the Old Testament calendar, such as Passover, the Feast of Tabernacles, and so on. While they may benefit those who are convicted about them, the New Testament doesn't require them for the Christian. But there are uniquely New Testament feasts that offer a setting for the retelling of the cross.

First of all, there's baptism. According to Romans 6, baptism is nothing less than a rehearsal of the death, burial, and resurrection of Jesus. Going into the water is like death. The person is then buried under the water and raised up out of it to a new life. Baptism is a rehearsal of the cross and the resurrection of Jesus Christ. So baptism celebrates the cross just as Passover memorialized the Exodus. We go down into the water just as Israel went down into the Red Sea. And whenever we rehearse the mighty acts of God, the power of the original act becomes real in the present.

That is why baptisms have such a powerful effect on those who observe. I have never performed a baptism without giving people in the audience a chance to indicate their own desire for baptism. One day in New York City 19 people stood up after such an appeal. Half of them I had never seen before. They were relatives and friends who had showed up to see somebody else get baptized. But when you rehearse the mighty acts of God, the power of the Resurrection is there. Sensing God's power and presence, they are moved to respond.

Another ceremony of the church is Communion, the Lord's Supper. According to 1 Corinthians 11:26, in the Lord's Supper we do show forth the Lord's death until He comes. Every time we celebrate the Lord's Supper we are rehearsing the death of Jesus Christ on the cross, providing tremendous opportunity for the power of the Spirit to work. By celebrating the "feasts of the church," such as baptism and the Lord's Supper, we can rehearse the mighty acts of God in a dramatic fashion.

3. Through Obedience

The Old Testament saints saw obedience as a way to rehearse the mighty acts of God. The same is true of the New Testament. In all of Paul's greatest letters he starts with the gospel, discussing what God has done in Jesus Christ. Then he uses the Greek word for "therefore," and follows the gospel with instruction in practical obedience. Let's look at Romans 12:1 as an example. "Therefore, I urge you, brothers, in view of God's mercy, to offer your bodies as living sacrifices, holy and pleasing to God." After knocking himself out to make the gospel as clear as possible in Romans 1-11, Paul says "therefore." The ideal response to the mighty act of God is to offer ourselves to God's service. We don't do it in order to earn salvation, but in grateful response to what He has already accomplished. Whether it has to do with what we eat, what we say, or what we do, true Christian obedience is related to the doing and dying of Jesus Christ.

Romans 14:23: "But the man who has doubts is condemned if he eats, because his eating is not from faith; and everything that does not come from faith is sin." Paul suggests that even good things done outside of a faith in the mighty acts of God become sin. It is through faith in them that obedience becomes a powerful thing. When we remember God's mighty deeds it motivates us to act like Him. We "do the right thing" in response to what He has already done.

4. In How We Treat People

In the Old Testament we noticed that people were to treat aliens the way that God had treated them in Egypt. God's actions toward us become the model for how we are to deal with other people. Matthew 25:40: "The King will reply, 'I tell you the truth, whatever you did for one of the least of these brothers of mine, you did for me.'" Through His sacrifice on the cross Jesus became identified with the human race. So when you visit a criminal in prison you're visiting Jesus. When you visit the sick you're visiting Jesus. And when you feed the hungry you're feeding Jesus. Through the gospel we learn how God responds to hurting people, to struggling people, to failing people. To God every person is intensely valuable, and He invites us to rehearse His mighty acts by behaving toward people the way He does.

Those days of my life when the gospel is most clear I feel as if I love everybody. But on days when the gospel is not so clear I have a tendency to despise "losers." The problem is, when I'm honest with myself, I'm the loser. And if there is no hope for "losers," then there is no hope for me. If I focus on myself, I become harder on myself and harder on others. But when I rehearse the mighty acts of God for me my screwed-up thought processes get turned around, and I can approach other people the way God does.

How does God want us to treat people who are totally messed up? Second Timothy 2:24-26: "And the Lord's servant must not quarrel; instead, he must be kind to everyone, able to teach, not resentful. Those who oppose him he must gently instruct, in the hope that God will grant them repentance leading them to a knowledge of the truth, and that they will come to their senses and escape from the trap of the devil, who has taken them captive to do his will." It takes a mighty act of God to change a heart. The practical issue is, How can we cooperate with God in reaching out to somebody totally screwed up? The text basically says to keep quiet. Instead of going in there to set them straight, you just show gentleness, kindness, teachableness, and humility. That's the ethics of rehearsing the mighty acts of God—it is dealing with other people the way God has already dealt with us.

5. Through the Routine Activities of Life

The key to avoiding the ups and downs in Christian experience is to bring the mighty acts of God constantly into the everyday routines of life. But how can we do that? Life for most people is an endless round of eating and drinking, waking and sleeping, working and resting. Very ordinary things. In themselves they make up a meaningless existence. We get a taste of this in Ecclesiastes 1:1-9. Everything is meaningless. People work day after day, but for what? The sun rises and sets; so what? The wind blows one way and then another, to no purpose. Everything is wearisome, and there is nothing new under the sun. Very depressing. And all those discouraging thoughts appear right in the middle of the Bible!

But the writer of Ecclesiastes is right. Life is boring on the whole. It is an endless round of routines with no particular meaning unless God does one of His mighty acts in our lives. First Peter 1:18,

19: "For you know that it was not with perishable things such as silver or gold that you were redeemed from the empty way of life handed down to you from your forefathers, but with the precious blood of Christ, a lamb without blemish or defect." Peter recognizes that the normal way of life is empty, meaningless. His solution is the precious blood of Christ. It is the mighty act of God on the cross that puts meaning into life, that gets rid of the emptiness. Whatever you do, tie it to the mighty actions of God in the past, the things He did for Israel and the things He has done for you. When you lay down this book and go back to your daily routines, do them in remembrance of Jesus.

As you sit down to eat, remember that rain, light, and sunshine would all have ceased with the entrance of sin if God had not been looking down the halls of history to the cross. So when you drink a glass of water remind yourself that Jesus is the water of life. When you're sitting at home and it is raining outside tell yourself that Jesus Christ is your shelter from the consequences of sin. And when you get dressed in the morning, put on the righteousness of Jesus Christ.

The New Testament is full of metaphors that can make everyday life meaningful. Just as God transformed some of the Canaanite routines in such a way as to remind His people of His mighty works, so the New Testament applies Christ to our daily lives today. When you go to sleep at night commit your life to God the way Jesus did on the cross: "Father, into Thy hands I commend My spirit." As you rise in the morning rehearse the resurrection of Jesus Christ and know that His mercy is new every morning.

At every wedding remember Ephesians 5, which speaks of the relationship of husband and wife as a type or symbol of that between Christ and the church. Or when you or someone you know gives birth to a child recite Isaiah 9:6, "Unto us a child is born, unto us a son is given" (KJV), and see it as a mighty act of God, the creation of new life!

Should you get sick, think of the one who bore our sicknesses and carried our sorrows (Isa. 53:4). Let suffering teach you He has suffered for you and will continue to suffer with you. And if time should last and you and I come to the end of life, we can still rejoice that the deteriorating body of sin and death is about to be destroyed, and that we will receive rest from the toil and the pain that come with life in a sinful world. Note the following priceless statement:

"To the death of Christ we owe even this earthly life. The bread we eat is the purchase of His broken body. The water we drink is bought by His spilled blood. Never one, saint or sinner, eats his daily food, but he is nourished by the body and the blood of Christ. The cross of Calvary is stamped on every loaf. It is reflected in every water spring. All this Christ has taught in appointing the emblems of His great sacrifice. The light shining from that Communion service in the upper chamber makes sacred the provisions for our daily life. The family board becomes as the table of the Lord, and every meal a sacrament. . . .

"Pride and self-worship cannot flourish in the soul that keeps fresh in memory the scenes of Calvary. He who beholds the Saviour's matchless love will be elevated in thought, purified in heart, transformed in character. He will go forth to be a light to the world, to reflect in some degree this mysterious love. The more we contemplate the cross of Christ, the more fully shall we adopt the language of the apostle when he said, 'God forbid that I should glory, save in the cross of our Lord Jesus Christ, by whom the world is crucified unto me, and I unto the world' (Gal. 6:14)" (*The Desire of Ages,* pp. 660, 661).

In this statement the cross of Christ becomes the sum and substance of all life and experience. As we bring the mighty act of God in Jesus Christ into continual consciousness, we become molded more and more into His image (2 Cor. 3:18). And we will also be preparing ourselves for the joys of eternal life, where rehearsing the mighty acts of God is a central part of human experience:

Revelation 5:12, 13: "In a loud voice they sang: 'Worthy is the Lamb, who was slain, to receive power and wealth and wisdom and strength and honor and glory and praise!' Then I heard every creature in heaven and on earth and under the earth and on the sea, and all that is in them, singing: 'To him who sits on the throne and to the Lamb be praise and honor and glory and power, for ever and ever!"

Rehearsing the cross, God's greatest and mightiest act, will be the science and the song of eternity. The difference between our life here and what we will experience there will be so great that we will never tire of singing the praises of the One who died for us and rose again on the third day. But why wait? We can begin to taste the glories of eternity here and now. You know the drill: "We were slaves in the land of Egypt . . ."